VEGETARIAN
BARBECUE
and summer cooking

Foreword by Rose Elliot

WINDWARD

House Editor: Julia Canning
Editor: Felicity Jackson
Art Editor: Caroline Dewing
Production: Richard Churchill
Contributors: Louise Steele, Linda Fraser and Felicity Jackson

Photographs: Paul Grater
Home Economist: Anne Hildyard
Stylist: Nova Pilbeam

Published by Windward, an imprint owned by
W.H. Smith & Son Limited
Registered No. 237811 England
Trading as WHS Distributors,
St John's House, East Street, Leicester LE1 6NE

© Marshall Cavendish Limited 1987

ISBN 0 7112 0462 4

Printed and bound in Italy by L.E.G.O.

Illustration on previous left-hand page:
Soya burgers (page 22) with Pepper relish
and Sweetcorn relish (page 38)
Illustration on following page:
Orange rice ring (page 75).

FOREWORD

'What do you do for a vegetarian barbecue?' is a question I'm often asked. Well, if you've ever wondered that, or if you're looking for some fresh new ideas for *al fresco* eating, here is your answer – or rather, more than 150 answers! *Vegetarian Barbecue and Summer Cooking* is a feast of colourful, light and pretty dishes for occasions ranging from barbecues and picnics to easy-going parties and informal entertaining.

So next time you want to have a meal in the garden, how about Camembert in vine leaves, grilled over charcoal, with hot Garlic bread? Or Barbecued lentil balls with Charcoalled pepper salad? To complete the meal there are mouthwatering ideas for sauces, relishes and drinks as well as some tempting desserts and cakes, such as Tipsy apple rings, Honey nut flapjacks (which my daughter can't wait for me to try) and an always-popular Carrot cake.

And there are many more exciting party dishes, any of which I'd be delighted to be offered! So I warmly recommend this book to you, and hope that you'll enjoy some memorable summer meals.

Rose Elliot

CONTENTS

INTRODUCTION

Some people see vegetarianism as a way of helping the world food situation – it takes far less land to produce food for a vegetarian diet than it does to graze cattle or grow fodder to feed them; the protein they provide is only a fraction of the amount of food they consume. Others are vegetarians because they cannot bear the killing of other creatures simply for food, or they dislike the methods involved in factory farming to produce meat at competitive prices.

Another reason for the growing popularity of the vegetarian diet is that the health experts stress that we should reduce the amount of fat we eat as this is a major cause of heart disease. In particular, they emphasize that we should cut down on saturated fat, which is found in animal products.

But because a vegetarian diet is healthy does not mean it has to be boring. This book shows you how a variety of delicious foods, including fruit, vegetables, nuts, cheese, eggs, cereals, pulses and seeds, can be used to create delicious, healthy meals.

Summer eating Here is a chance for vegetarians to enjoy all the pleasures of summer entertaining, barbecues and picnics with recipes designed to make full use of fresh summer produce. There are new ideas for old familiar favourites like strawberries, peaches, peas and beans, as well as exciting ways to use more exotic ingredients like passionfruit, mangoes, vine leaves and radicchio.

Barbecues Barbecues traditionally consist of meat, but it's just as easy to prepare a vegetarian barbecue. Peppers, mushrooms and corn cobs are just a few of the vegetables that taste delicious wrapped in aluminium foil and cooked over the fire. All the natural juices are retained and the food has a wonderful flavour. Burgers can be made from soya beans, lentils, rice or potatoes. All kinds of vegetables can be cooked on skewers and basted with olive oil, a marinade or a sauce. Fruit can be cooked the same way with a little alcohol, or flambéed after barbecuing.

Picnics There is more to picnics than egg sandwiches, and the picnic chapter has a wealth of ideas for turning every picnic into a feast. There are dishes the children will love and the adults won't be able to resist.

Salads Salads are an important part of any vegetarian diet so there are ideas for main meal salads as well as side salads and starters.

Entertaining The entertaining chapter shows you how to use fresh fruit and vegetables to best advantage to create summer soups, pâtés, dips, finger and fork food and irresistible desserts. There are also drinks to suit any summer occasion from barbecues and picnics, informal lunches and brunches to sophisticated cocktail parties.

BARBECUES

The tempting aroma and the sight of food sizzling over the fire whets the appetite and explains why barbecuing is becoming more and more popular. It also means the cook is not tied to the kitchen stove away from the guests.

There are many different types of barbecues, ranging from small, cheap, portable ones such as the hibachi to the sophisticated, expensive gas and electric barbecues. If you cook outdoors regularly, it is worth building a permanent barbecue in the garden, well away from fences and trees.

Barbecue accessories

The most useful items are a set of long-handled tools including tongs, fork, skewers and basting brush (bristle not nylon). A long-handled hinged wire grill is good for cooking several small items at the same time as they can be turned easily.

Aluminium foil is essential for cooking parcelled vegetables and fruit; a double layer of ordinary kitchen foil or heavy duty foil can be used equally successfully.

Oven gloves are needed for handling hot foil parcels and metal skewers, and it is a good idea to have a small water sprinkler near by in case you need to douse flames.

Fuel

The most common forms of fuel are lumpwood charcoal or the longer burning uniformly-shaped charcoal briquettes.

Start the fire with solid or liquid fire lighters or an electric fire lighter – never petrol, methylated spirits or cigarette lighter fuel. Specially impregnated charcoal briquettes are available, but they are more expensive.

Light the fire about 30-45 minutes before you want to start cooking. Unless using self-starting briquettes, build a pyramid shape of charcoal, placing pieces of fire lighter in the pyramid. If using liquid fire lighter, squirt it over the charcoal, leave to soak in for a couple of minutes, then light the charcoal. Do not use a liquid fire lighter once the charcoal has been lit or it may flare up. If the charcoal looks as if it needs rekindling, use pieces of solid fire lighter.

The barbecue is ready for cooking when the charcoal is covered in grey-white ash and it is impossible to hold your hand over the fire for more than about 3 seconds. It is important to wait until this stage. Spread the charcoal over the grate and start cooking.

The heat can be increased by knocking the ash off the charcoal and pushing the pieces closer together – or spread the charcoal out to lower the heat.

If you are planning a long cooking session, you will probably need to add more charcoal. To do this without lowering the heat, place pieces of charcoal around the edge to warm, then move them into the centre of the fire.

Adding fresh herbs, garlic cloves or orange zest to the fire gives food an aromatic flavour.

Cooking the food

Most foods should be cooked on the grill over the fire, but some items can be wrapped in aluminium foil and cooked in the coals.

Vegetarian burgers tend to be softer than meat ones, although Soya burgers (see page 22) are firm enough to cook on the barbecue grill. Others are best cooked on an oiled, heated metal tray placed on the grill, to prevent them breaking up.

Stuffed peppers

PARCELLED FOOD

Food cooked in a parcel on the barbecue has all the natural juices and flavour sealed in. Vine leaves are perfect for wrapping round small items like slices of Camembert while larger foods like corn cobs, and courgettes need to be wrapped in a double layer of aluminium foil.

Paprika corn parcels

Serves 4

100 g/4 oz butter, softened

½ teaspoon paprika

½ small onion, finely chopped

4 corn cobs

2 tablespoons chopped chives

1 Prepare the barbecue. Cut out 4 large pieces of double thickness foil.
2 In a small bowl, mix together the butter, paprika and onion. Place one corn cob on each piece of foil and spread the butter over them, dividing it equally between the cobs. Sprinkle chopped chives over the top.
3 Roll up the corn cobs in the foil, folding the sides to seal the parcels tightly.
4 When the charcoal has reached the white ash stage cook, the parcels in the coals for 15-20 minutes until the corn is tender.
5 Unwrap the corn cobs, transfer to a serving dish and pour over the juices from the parcels.

Stuffed peppers

Serves 4

225 g/8 oz fresh or frozen peas, podded weight if fresh

4 red, green or yellow peppers

50 g/2 oz butter

1 onion, chopped

2 tablespoons finely chopped fresh mint

2 eggs, beaten

salt and freshly ground black pepper

vegetable oil, for brushing

1 Prepare the barbecue. Cut out 4 large pieces of double thickness foil.
2 Cook the peas in boiling water until tender. Drain well.
3 Meanwhile, cut a slice from the stalk end of each pepper and reserve. Cut a thin slice from the other end to allow the pepper to stand upright. Scoop out the seeds.
4 Melt the butter in a saucepan, add the onion and fry gently for 5 minutes until soft. Remove from the heat and allow to cool slightly.
5 Purée the onion and peas in a blender or food processor, then stir in the mint and beaten eggs and season to taste with salt and pepper.
6 Spoon the mixture into the peppers and replace the lids. Stand each pepper on a piece of foil and brush with oil.
7 Fold up the edges of the foil to seal the parcels tightly and when the charcoal has reached the white ash stage cook the parcels in the coals for 30-40 minutes until the peppers are tender and the filling has set.

Avocado mushrooms

Serves 6

6 large flat mushrooms, wiped

1 avocado

2 teaspoons lemon juice

few drops of Tabasco sauce

salt and freshly ground black pepper

50 g/2 oz Cheddar cheese, grated

½ canned pimiento, drained, cut into 6 strips

1 Prepare the barbecue. Cut out 6 pieces of double thickness aluminium foil.

2 Gently twist out the mushroom stalks and finely chop.

3 Cut the avocado in half, peel and remove the stone. Mash the avocado in a small bowl with the lemon juice, then stir in the mushroom stalks, Tabasco sauce and salt and pepper to taste.

4 Place one mushroom, gill side up, on each piece of foil and spoon the avocado mixture on to the mushrooms.

5 Sprinkle the grated cheese over the top. Cut each pimiento strip in half and arrange 2 pieces in a cross on each mushroom.

6 Fold up the edges of the foil to seal the parcels tightly. When the charcoal has reached the white ash stage, cook on the barbecue grill for 10-15 minutes.

7 Unwrap the parcels, transfer the mushrooms to a serving dish and then top with the juices from the foil.

Baked potatoes

Serves 4

4 × 225 g/8 oz potatoes, scrubbed

vegetable oil, for brushing

1 Prepare the barbecue.

2 When the coals have reached the white ash stage, prick the potatoes with a fork and brush with oil.

3 Put each potato on a piece of double thickness foil and seal the parcels tightly. Place on the barbecue grill and cook for 45-60 minutes until tender.

4 Unwrap potatoes and transfer to a serving dish. Split them open and serve with butter, grated cheese or one of the fillings below.

Creamy egg filling

Serves 4

4 eggs, hard-boiled

150 ml/¼ pint soured cream

few drops of Tabasco sauce

salt and freshly ground black pepper

1 tablespoon toasted sesame seeds (black if possible)

1 Slice the hard-boiled eggs and mix into the soured cream. Add the Tabasco sauce and season to taste with salt and pepper.

2 Spoon into the cooked potatoes and sprinkle with toasted sesame seeds.

Curried mung bean filling

Serves 4

100 g/4 oz mung beans

450 ml/¾ pint water

½-1 teaspoon curry powder

6 tablespoons mango chutney, chopped

1 Wash the beans in several changes of cold water, then place in a saucepan with the water. Bring to the boil and simmer for 15-20 minutes until the beans are tender and most of the liquid has been absorbed.

2 Stir in curry powder and cook gently for 1-2 minutes. Stir in mango chutney and serve.

Camembert in vine leaves

Serves 6

225 g/8 oz packet vine leaves in brine

225 g/8 oz Camembert

olive oil, for brushing

1 Prepare the barbecue.
2 Drain the vine leaves, place in a large bowl and pour boiling water over them. Leave to soak for 20 minutes until softened.
3 Drain the leaves, then soak in cold water for a further 20 minutes. Drain well and pat dry with absorbent kitchen paper.
4 Cut the Camembert into the same number of slices as there are vine leaves (approximately 24).
5 Place the vine leaves, shiny side down, on a work surface and place a piece of Camembert in the centre of each leaf. Fold over the top and sides to make a parcel.
6 Brush with olive oil, then when the charcoal has reached the white ash stage place the parcels in a greased hinged grill. Cook on the barbecue grill for 2-3 minutes, then turn the hinged grill over and cook the other side for 2-3 minutes until the vine leaves are crispy and the cheese melted.

Garlic bread

Serves 6

2 baguettes or 1 large French loaf

100 g/4 oz butter, softened

2-3 garlic cloves, crushed

salt and freshly ground black pepper

1 Prepare the barbecue. Cut out 2 large pieces of double thickness aluminium foil (or one very large piece if using a French loaf).
2 Slice the loaves or loaf diagonally into 2 cm/½ inch slices, leaving the slices joined at the base.
3 In a small bowl, mix the butter and garlic until well blended. Season to taste with salt and pepper.
4 Spread the garlic butter over each side of the bread slices.
5 Place one loaf on each piece of foil and fold up the edges to secure the parcels tightly.
6 When the charcoal has reached the white ash stage, place the parcels on the barbecue grill and heat for 20-25 minutes.
7 Unwrap the parcels and transfer the loaves to a serving dish. Cut through the slices to separate them and serve at once.

Variation

◆ To make herb bread: omit the garlic and add 2 tablespoons finely chopped fresh herbs to the softened butter. Heat on the barbecue in the same way as Garlic bread.

Camembert in vine leaves

Mozzarella tomatoes

Serves 6

6 large tomatoes

75 g/3 oz Mozzarella cheese, cut into 6 pieces

2 tablespoons finely chopped fresh basil

parsley sprigs, to garnish

1 Prepare the barbecue. Cut out 6 pieces of double thickness aluminium foil.

2 Cut the tops off the tomatoes; insert a small, sharp pointed knife and cut all the way round the tomato cutting in a zig zag pattern. Reserve the tops. Scoop out the flesh from the tomatoes and fill with a slice of Mozzarella. Sprinkle chopped basil over the cheese, then replace the tomato lids.

3 Place one tomato on each piece of foil, then fold up the edges of the foil to seal the parcel tightly.

4 When the charcoal has reached the white ash stage, cook the parcels on the barbecue grill for 10-15 minutes until the tomatoes are heated through and the cheese melted.

5 Carefully unwrap the parcels and transfer the tomatoes to a serving dish. Place a small sprig of parsley on each tomato lid and serve at once.

Rice-filled courgettes

Serves 6

6 large courgettes

olive oil, for brushing

parsley sprigs and lemon twists, to garnish

FILLING

1 tablespoon olive oil

1 onion, finely chopped

100 g/4 oz tomatoes, chopped

2 tablespoons chopped fresh parsley

100 g/4 oz cooked brown rice

4 allspice berries, crushed

2 tablespoons pine nuts

salt and freshly ground black pepper

1 Prepare the barbecue. Cut out 6 large pieces of double thickness aluminium foil.

2 Cut the courgettes in half lengthways and scoop out the seeds. Brush the courgette skins with oil and arrange 2 halves on each piece of foil.

3 Make the filling: heat the oil in a saucepan, add the onion and cook for 5 minutes until soft.

4 Remove from the heat and stir in the remaining ingredients, seasoning to taste with salt and pepper. Mix well.

5 Spoon the filling into the courgette halves, pressing down with the back of a spoon.

6 Fold up the edges of the foil to seal the parcel tightly and when the charcoal has reached the white ash stage cook on the barbecue grill for 20-30 minutes until the courgettes are tender.

7 Unwrap the parcels and transfer the courgettes to a serving platter. Garnish with parsley sprigs and lemon twists.

Celery and mushroom parcels

Serves 4

8 large celery stalks

25 g/1 oz butter

100 g/4 oz mushrooms, finely chopped

1 garlic clove, chopped

25 g/1 oz wholemeal breadcrumbs

1 teaspoon soy sauce

few drops of Tabasco sauce

salt and freshly ground black pepper

whole chives, for tying

1 Prepare the barbecue. Cut out a large piece of double thickness aluminium foil.

2 Cut a 12.5cm/5 inch length from the thick end of each of the celery stalks (reserve the remainder for a salad).

3 Melt the butter in a saucepan, add the mushrooms and garlic and fry gently for 5 minutes until soft. Stir in the breadcrumbs, soy sauce and Tabasco and mix well. Season to taste with salt and pepper.

4 Spoon the mushroom mixture on to 4 of the celery stalks, dividing it equally between them, then place the remaining celery stalks on top. Tie up each celery parcel with 3 chives (or fine thread if chives are unavailable).

5 Place the celery parcels in a single layer on the foil and fold up the edges of the foil to secure the foil parcel tightly.

6 When the coals have reached the white ash stage, place the foil parcel on the barbecue grill and cook for 20-25 minutes, turning the parcel over halfway through.

7 Unwrap the celery parcels and transfer to a serving dish.

◆ These parcels make a good starter – they can be eaten while the main course is being cooked. If preferred, the celery can be cut into small, bite-sized pieces for hot nibbles to have with drinks before the meal.

Baked stuffed avocados

Serves 4

25 g/1 oz bulgar wheat

2 firm avocados

50 g/2 oz blue Stilton

25 g/1 oz walnuts, finely chopped

salt and freshly ground black pepper

brown bread and butter, to serve

1 Put the bulgar wheat in a bowl and pour over enough boiling water to cover. Leave to soak for 45 minutes.

2 Meanwhile, prepare the barbecue and cut out 4 pieces of double thickness aluminium foil.

3 Drain the bulgar wheat in a sieve, pressing well to squeeze out all the excess water.

4 In a small bowl, mash the Stilton, then stir in the bulgar wheat and walnuts. Season to taste with salt and pepper.

5 Cut the avocados in half and remove the stones. Spoon the cheese mixture into each of the avocado hollows.

6 Place one avocado half on each piece of foil and fold up the edges to secure the parcel tightly. When the charcoal has reached the white ash stage, place the parcels on the barbecue grill and cook for 15-20 minutes.

7 Unwrap the parcels and transfer the avocado halves to a serving dish. Serve with slices of brown bread and butter.

GRILL-TOP FOOD

This section includes kebabs, burgers and grilled vegetables. When barbecuing kebabs, choose firm, fresh vegetables that won't break up when threaded on skewers. Soya and lentil mixtures should be well chilled before grilling. Potato and rice mixes are best cooked on a heated, oiled metal sheet.

Marinated kebabs

Serves 6

2 red peppers, deseeded and cut into 2.5 cm/1 inch squares

36 baby corn

6 onions, each cut into 6 wedges

48 bay leaves

vegetable oil, for greasing

MARINADE

125 ml/4 fl oz olive oil

2 tablespoons cider vinegar

2 teaspoons chopped fresh tarragon

2 garlic cloves, crushed

1 tablespoon juniper berries, crushed

salt and freshly ground black pepper

1 Thread 12 flat skewers with the pepper squares, baby corn, onion wedges and bay leaves, arranging them alternately. Place the kebabs in a large shallow dish.
2 In a small bowl, mix together the marinade ingredients, then pour over the kebabs. Leave to marinate for 2-3 hours, turning occasionally and basting with the marinade.
3 Meanwhile, prepare the barbecue.
4 When the charcoal has reached the white ash stage, drain the kebabs, reserving the marinade.
5 Brush the barbecue grill with oil. Arrange the kebabs on the grid and grill for 10-15 minutes, turning frequently and basting with the marinade.

Variation
◆ Replace the red peppers with one yellow pepper, cut into squares, and 3 limes, cut into wedges.

Marinated kebab and Sweet and sour kebab

Sweet and sour kebabs

Serves 6

4 round slices of fresh pineapple, 1 cm/½ inch thick, peeled and cored

4 courgettes, each cut into 6 slices

24 cherry tomatoes

2 green peppers, deseeded and cut into 2.5 cm/1 inch squares

vegetable oil, for greasing

SWEET AND SOUR SAUCE

2 teaspoons potato flour or cornflour

6 tablespoons water

1 tablespoon lemon juice

3 tablespoons orange juice

3 tablespoons white wine vinegar

4 tablespoons dark soft brown sugar

1 teaspoon soy sauce

salt

1 Prepare the barbecue.
2 Make the sauce: in a small bowl, blend the potato flour with the water until smooth. Stir in the remaining sauce ingredients, seasoning to taste with salt.
3 Bring to the boil in a small saucepan. Reduce the heat and simmer for 5 minutes.
4 Cut each pineapple round into 6 wedges.
5 Thread 12 flat skewers with the pineapple, courgettes, tomatoes and pepper.
6 At white ash stage, brush grill with oil.
7 Arrange the kebabs on the grill, brush with the sauce and grill for 10-15 minutes, turning the skewers frequently and basting with the sauce.

Variation
◆ Use 2 lemons, cut into wedges, instead of the tomatoes.

Soya burgers

Makes 12

225 g/8 oz soya beans, soaked overnight

1 onion, finely chopped

50 g/2 oz mushrooms, chopped

½ green pepper, deseeded and chopped

1 tablespoon chopped fresh mint

1 tablespoon chopped fresh sage

4 tablespoons tomato purée

¼ teaspoon chilli powder

1 egg, beaten

175 g/6 oz cooked brown rice

vegetable oil, for brushing

1 Drain the beans and put in a saucepan. Cover with cold water, bring to the boil and boil for 10 minutes. Reduce the heat and simmer for 3-3½ hours until tender. Drain thoroughly.

2 Allow to cool slightly, then mince the beans. Put the beans in a bowl and mix in the remaining ingredients.

3 Shape the mixture into 12 burgers, arrange on a plate and chill in the refrigerator for at least 30 minutes.

4 Meanwhile, prepare the barbecue.

5 When the charcoal has reached the white ash stage, brush the barbecue grill with oil. Brush the burgers with oil and place on the grill. Grill for 15-20 minutes, turning once, until browned on both sides.

◆ Serve with Fresh tomato sauce (see page 36) or Chilli sauce (see page 34).

◆ For 175 g/6 oz cooked brown rice, you will need to cook 50 g/2 oz raw rice.

Spicy kebabs

Serves 6

36 small cauliflower florets

36 button mushrooms

6 courgettes, each cut into 6 slices

36 bay leaves

vegetable oil, for brushing

SPICY MARINADE

300 ml/½ pint natural yoghurt

1 cm/½ inch piece of root ginger, peeled and finely chopped

¼ teaspoon ground cardamom

¼ teaspoon cayenne pepper

1 tablespoon chopped parsley

1 garlic clove, crushed

salt and freshly ground black pepper

1 Make the marinade: combine all the ingredients in a large shallow bowl and stir well.

2 Thread 12 flat skewers with the cauliflower florets, button mushrooms, courgettes and bay leaves, arranging them alternately.

3 Arrange the kebabs in the shallow bowl and spoon the marinade over the top. Leave to marinate for 2-3 hours, turning the skewers occasionally and basting with the marinade.

4 Meanwhile, prepare the barbecue.

5 When the charcoal has reached the white ash stage, drain the kebabs, reserving the marinade.

6 Brush the barbecue grill with oil. Arrange the kebabs on the grill and cook for 10-15 minutes, turning the skewers frequently and basting with the marinade.

Rice and nut burgers

Makes 6

25 g/1 oz butter

1 onion, finely chopped

100 g/4 oz button mushrooms, chopped

350 g/12 oz cooked brown rice

50 g/2 oz chopped nuts

1 tablespoon tomato purée

few drops of Tabasco sauce

salt and freshly ground black pepper

1 egg, beaten

vegetable oil, for greasing

1 Prepare the barbecue.

2 Meanwhile, melt the butter in a saucepan, add the onion and fry gently for 5 minutes until soft. Add the mushrooms and fry for a further 2 minutes.

3 Stir in the rice, nuts, tomato purée, Tabasco and seasoning. Mix well, then stir in the beaten egg.

4 Divide the mixture into 6 portions and shape each into a round burger-shape. Spread out the breadcrumbs on a flat plate and dip the burgers in the crumbs until well coated. Arrange them on a plate and refrigerate until well chilled.

5 When the charcoal has reached the white ash stage, heat an oiled metal sheet on the barbecue grill. Place the burgers on the sheet and cook for 10-15 minutes, turning once, until browned on both sides.

Barbecued chips

Serves 4

500 g/1 lb potatoes, sliced into 5 mm/¼ inch thick chips

4 tablespoons olive oil

3 onions, chopped

1 Prepare the barbecue.

2 Bring a saucepan of water to the boil, add the chips and cook for 2 minutes, then drain and rinse under cold running water. Drain and pat dry on absorbent paper. Set aside.

3 When the charcoal has reached the white ash stage, heat the oil in a frying pan over the coals.

4 Add the onion and cook for 20-25 minutes until very brown. Add the chips and cook for a further 10 minutes until the chips are tender.

◆ Chips cooked this way have a lovely flavour both from the barbecue and the onions.

◆ Serve the chips with the Soya burgers (see page 22) or the Rice and nut burgers (left), or with any of the vegetable kebabs.

Barbecued lentil balls

Makes 16

225 g/8 oz split red lentils

1 teaspoon olive oil, plus extra for brushing

1 tablespoon chopped fresh sorrel (optional)

1 tablespoon chopped fresh parsley

1 egg, beaten

2 tablespoons tahini (sesame cream)

50 g/2 oz wholemeal breadcrumbs

100 g/4 oz Cheddar cheese, grated

salt and freshly ground black pepper

parsley sprigs, to garnish

COATING

1 egg, beaten

100 g/4 oz wholemeal breadcrumbs

1 Rinse the lentils in several changes of cold water, then place in a saucepan with 3 times their volume of water and the teaspoon of oil. Bring to the boil, reduce the heat and simmer for 15-20 minutes until the lentils are tender and the water has evaporated.

2 Beat the lentils with a wooden spoon until smooth, then leave until cold.

3 When the lentils are cold, mix in the remaining ingredients and shape the mixture into 16 balls.

4 Put the beaten egg in a shallow dish and spread out the breadcrumbs on a flat plate. Dip the lentil balls into the beaten egg, then into the breadcrumbs making sure they are completely coated. Arrange in a single layer on a plate and chill in the refrigerator for 1-2 hours.

5 Meanwhile, prepare the barbecue.

6 When the charcoal has reached the white ash stage, brush the barbecue grill with oil. Place the lentil balls on the grill and cook for 8-10 minutes, turning frequently, until lightly browned on all sides.

7 Transfer to a serving dish, garnish with parsley sprigs and serve.

Cheesy potato cakes

Makes 6

350 g/12 oz potatoes, quartered

15 g/½ oz butter

1 onion, finely chopped

100 g/4 oz Cheddar cheese, grated

salt and freshly ground black pepper

50 g/2 oz wholemeal breadcrumbs

vegetable oil, for greasing

TO SERVE

fresh chives

soured cream

1 Cook the potatoes in lightly salted boiling water until tender. Mash them, then heat very gently to evaporate any moisture. Leave to cool.

2 Meanwhile, melt the butter in a saucepan, add the chopped onion and fry gently for 5 minutes until soft.

3 Mix the onion into the mashed potato with the cheese. Season to taste with salt and pepper.

4 Divide the mixture into 6 portions and shape into round cakes (handle as little as possible as the mixture is very soft).

5 Spread out the breadcrumbs on a plate and dip the potato cakes into the crumbs, pressing them on firmly, until well coated. Arrange on a plate and refrigerate until chilled.

6 Meanwhile, prepare the barbecue.

7 When the charcoal has reached the white ash stage, heat an oiled metal sheet on the barbecue grill. Add the potato cakes and cook for 5-10 minutes until browned on both sides.

8 Transfer to a serving dish and garnish with chives. Serve with soured cream.

◆ It is essential that the potato cakes are thoroughly chilled; the mixture is so soft before chilling that the cakes will break up if cooked without chilling. For this reason they are best cooked on a metal sheet rather than directly on the barbecue grill.

Cheesy potato cakes

Charcoalled pepper salad

Serves 6

2 green peppers

2 red peppers

2 yellow peppers

vegetable oil, for greasing

fresh fennel leaves, to garnish

DRESSING

4 tablespoons olive oil

2 teaspoons lemon juice

1 garlic clove, crushed

salt and freshly ground black pepper

1 Prepare the barbecue.

2 Make the dressing: put all the dressing ingredients in a bowl or screw-topped jar and whisk or shake until well combined.

3 When the charcoal is at the white ash stage, thread the peppers on to flat skewers. Oil the barbecue grill and place the peppers on the grill.

4 Grill the peppers, turning frequently, until their skins blister and go black all over.

5 Immediately, plunge them into a bowl of cold water and leave for 2 minutes. The skins will then peel off easily.

6 Slice the peeled peppers in half widthways and scrape out the seeds. Cut a thin ring from each half and set aside.

7 Slice the remaining part of the peppers into thick wedges and arrange in groups of alternating colours on a serving dish.

8 Make a slit in each of the reserved pepper rings and link them together, alternating the colours, then arrange on top of the pepper wedges (if preferred, make 2 circles of 6 rings each).

9 Pour over the dressing and serve at once, garnished with fresh fennel leaves.

Garlicky aubergine slices

Makes 9-10 slices

50 g/2 oz butter

2-3 garlic cloves, crushed

50 g/2 oz wholemeal breadcrumbs

225 g/8 oz aubergine, cut into 9 or 10 slices about 7 mm/⅓ inch thick

40 g/1½ oz Parmesan cheese, grated

olive oil, for frying

1 Prepare the barbecue.

2 Melt the butter in a saucepan, add the garlic and fry gently for 1 minute. Stir in the breadcrumbs and fry gently until well browned and crisp, but not burnt. Set aside.

3 Heat 4 tablespoons olive oil in a frying pan, add the aubergine slices and fry over medium heat for 5-10 minutes, turning once. Add more olive oil as necessary.

4 Remove the aubergine slices from the pan and spoon the garlicky breadcrumbs on top, dividing them equally between the slices. Sprinkle the Parmesan cheese over the top of the crumbs.

5 When the charcoal has reached the white ash stage, oil the barbecue grill and arrange the aubergine slices on the grill. Cook for about 5 minutes until the crumb topping is hot.

FIRE FRUITS

Barbecued fruits are a perfect way to round off a meal in the garden. They don't need fierce heat so parcelled fruit can be placed at the edge of the fire to cook slowly.
Cook fruit kebabs just long enough to caramelize a sugary coating, and add alcohol of your choice to parcelled fruits.

Brandied baked apples

Serves 4

1 orange

50 g/2 oz dried fruit

good pinch of freshly grated nutmeg

2 tablespoons brandy

4 large cooking apples

15 g/½ oz butter

2 tablespoons dark soft brown sugar

double or pouring cream, to serve

1 Cut out 4 pieces of double thickness aluminium foil large enough to parcel apples.

2 Grate the zest from half the orange and pare the zest from the other half. Cut the pared zest into very thin julienne strips. Place in a small saucepan and cover with water. Bring to the boil and simmer for 5 minutes until tender. Drain and rinse under cold water. Set aside for decoration.

3 Put the dried fruit, nutmeg and grated zest into a small bowl, pour over the brandy and leave to soak for at least 30 minutes – preferably several hours.

4 Meanwhile, prepare the barbecue.

5 When the charcoal has reached the white ash stage, core the apples to within 1 cm/½ inch of the base (this prevents the stuffing falling out during cooking), then make a shallow cut through the skin around the middle of each apple.

6 Stand the apples on the pieces of foil and spoon the fruit mixture into the centre of the apples. Mix the butter and sugar together and dot the filling with the mixture.

7 Fold up the edges of the foil to seal the parcels tightly. Cook on the barbecue grill for 40-50 minutes until the apples are tender.

8 Carefully unwrap the parcels and transfer the apples to a serving dish. Sprinkle the reserved orange zest strips over the top and serve at once with cream.

Caramel-topped oranges

Serves 6

6 oranges

1 tablespoon rose water

1 tablespoon Cointreau

3 tablespoons caster sugar

40 g/1½ oz butter, cut into 6 pieces

CARAMEL TOPPING

100 g/4 oz granulated sugar

150 ml/¼ pint water

vegetable oil, for greasing

1 Make the caramel topping: grease a baking tray and put the sugar and water into a small, heavy-based saucepan. Heat gently, without stirring, until the sugar has dissolved, then bring to the boil and boil for 5 minutes or until the syrup turns a deep golden colour.

2 Immediately pour into the greased baking tray to make a thin layer. Allow it to become completely cold, then crack the set caramel with the side of a spoon or a rolling pin to form fine chips. Set aside for decoration.

3 Prepare the barbecue. Cut out 6 large pieces of double thickness aluminium foil.

4 Peel the oranges over a bowl, using a sharp knife. Make sure all the pith is removed and reserve any juice that is squeezed out.

5 Slice each orange horizontally into rounds, then reassemble in the shape of the oranges. Place one orange on each piece of foil. Mix together the reserved orange juice, rose water and liqueur and pour over the oranges, dividing it equally between them. Sprinkle the sugar over the oranges and top each with a piece of butter.

6 Fold up the edges of the foil to seal the parcels tightly. When the charcoal has reached the white ash stage, cook the oranges on the grill for 15-20 minutes.

7 Carefully unwrap the parcels, transfer the oranges to a serving dish, sprinkle over the caramel chips and serve at once.

Gingered pears

Serves 4

4 firm pears

2 pieces preserved stem ginger, finely chopped

4 tablespoons ginger syrup

TO SERVE

double cream

crisp sweet biscuits

1 Prepare the barbecue. Cut out 4 large pieces of double thickness aluminium foil.

2 Peel the pears, cut in half and remove the cores. Place 2 halves on each piece of foil. Fill the centres with the chopped stem ginger, dividing it equally between them, and pour the syrup over the top.

3 Fold up the edges of the foil to secure the parcels tightly.

4 When the charcoal has reached the white ash stage, place the parcels on the barbecue grill and cook for 20-25 minutes.

5 Unwrap the parcels and transfer the pears to a serving dish. Serve with cream and biscuits.

Caramel-topped oranges

Spicy fruit kebabs

Serves 6
2 oranges
2 dessert apples
2 firm pears
1 tablespoon lemon juice
2 peaches
100 g/4 oz black or green grapes or a mixture of the two
BUTTER SAUCE
100 g/4 oz butter
1 tablespoon dark soft brown sugar
1 teaspoon ground cinnamon
good pinch freshly grated nutmeg
1 tablespoon apple juice

1 Prepare the barbecue.

2 Meanwhile, peel the oranges and remove the pith with a sharp knife. Divide each orange into 6 wedges.

3 Cut the apples in half and remove the cores. Cut each half into 3 wedges. Cut the pears in half, remove the cores, then cut into thick chunks. Dip the apples and the pears in the lemon juice.

4 Cut the peaches in half and remove the stones. Cut each half into 3 pieces.

5 Thread all the fruits on to 6 flat metal skewers, arranging the pieces alternately.

6 Make the sauce: melt the butter in a small saucepan, then stir in the sugar, cinnamon, nutmeg and apple juice. Heat gently, stirring, until well blended.

7 When the coals have reached the white ash stage, place the skewers on the barbecue grill and baste with the butter sauce. Grill them, turning frequently, for about 5 minutes until the sugary coating begins to caramelize.

8 Transfer the fruit to a serving dish and serve at once.

Jamaican bananas

Serves 6
6 firm bananas
2 tablespoons lemon juice
6 tablespoons rum
6 tablespoons dark soft brown sugar
ground cinnamon, for sprinkling
40 g/1½ oz butter, cut into 6 pieces
whipped cream to serve

1 Prepare the barbecue. Cut out 6 large pieces of double thickness aluminium foil.

2 When the charcoal has reached the white ash stage, peel the bananas and place one on each piece of foil.

3 Brush each banana with 1 teaspoon lemon juice, then pour over 1 tablespoon rum. Sprinkle each one with 1 tablespoon sugar and a sprinkling of cinnamon and dot with butter.

4 Fold up the edges of the foil to seal the parcels tightly and cook on the barbecue grill for 5-10 minutes.

5 Carefully unwrap the parcels and transfer the bananas to a serving dish. Pour over the juices from the parcel and serve at once with whipped cream.

Flambéed fruit kebabs

Serves 6

2 round slices of fresh pineapple, 1 cm/½ inch thick, peeled and cored

3 very firm bananas

12 firm red cherries

3 nectarines, stoned and quartered

50 g/2 oz caster sugar

1-2 teaspoons ground cinnamon

2 tablespoons rum or brandy

1 Prepare the barbecue.

2 When the charcoal has reached the white ash stage, cut each pineapple round into 6 wedges. Peel the bananas and cut each one into 4 pieces.

3 Thread 6 flat skewers with the pineapple cubes, cherries, bananas and nectarine pieces, arranging them alternately.

4 Mix together the sugar and cinnamon and sprinkle the mixture over the kebabs. Place the kebabs on the barbecue grill and cook for 5 minutes, turning frequently, until the coating is caramelized.

5 Transfer the fruit to a serving dish. Heat the rum or brandy in a warm ladle, ignite it and pour, still flaming, over the fruit. Serve at once.

Tipsy apple rings

Serves 4-6

4 cooking apples

pouring cream, to serve

vegetable oil, for greasing

REDCURRANT GLAZE

8 tablespoons redcurrant jelly

1 teaspoon finely grated orange zest

2 tablespoons port

1 Prepare the barbecue.

2 Make the glaze: put the redcurrant jelly, orange zest and port in a small, heavy-based saucepan. Bring to the boil, stirring, and simmer for 2-3 minutes until thick.

3 Peel and core the apples and slice horizontally into 7 mm/⅓ inch thick rings. Brush with the glaze.

4 When the charcoal has reached the white ash stage, oil the barbecue grill and place the apple slices on it. Grill for 5 minutes on each side basting with the glaze. If you have a hinged grill, place the apple slices, a few at a time, in it. They can then be turned all at once.

5 Transfer the rings to a serving dish and serve immediately with cream poured over them.

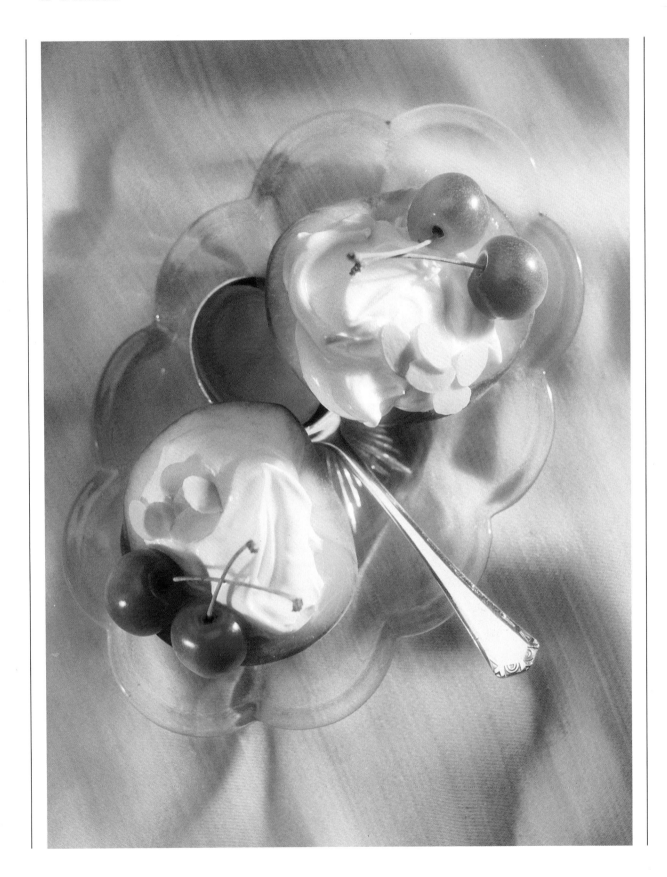

Barbecued peaches

Serves 4

4 peaches, halved and stoned

4 fresh or glacé cherries, halved

4 teaspoons caster sugar

8 teaspoons kirsch

25 g/1 oz flaked almonds, toasted

fresh or glacé cherries, to decorate

LIQUEUR CREAM

250 ml/8 fl oz double cream

2 tablespoons kirsch

2 tablespoons icing sugar

1 Make the liqueur cream: whip the cream until softly peaking, then fold in the kirsch and icing sugar. Refrigerate until ready to serve.

2 Prepare the barbecue. Cut out 4 large pieces of double thickness aluminium foil.

3 Place 2 peach halves on each piece of foil and place a half cherry in the centre of each. Sprinkle 1 teaspoon of sugar over each parcel and pour 2 teaspoons kirsch over each.

4 Fold up the edges of the foil to seal the parcel tightly. When the charcoal has reached the white ash stage, place the parcels on the grill and cook for 10-20 minutes until the peaches are warm.

5 Unwrap the parcels and transfer the peaches to a serving dish. Pour over the juices from the parcel and top with the liqueur cream. Scatter over the toasted almonds, decorate with the cherries and serve.

◆ Leaving the skins on the peaches turns the cooking juices a pretty pale pink, but if preferred the skins can be removed before cooking. To peel: put the peaches in a bowl, pour over boiling water and leave for 30 seconds, then the skins will peel off easily.

Apricot pastries

Makes 10

225 g/8 oz plain flour

100 g/4 oz butter, diced

2 tablespoons water

1-2 teaspoons rose water

5 teaspoons apricot conserve

icing sugar, for dusting

1 Sift the flour into a bowl, add the butter and rub in until the mixture resembles breadcrumbs. Add the water and rose water, sprinkling it over the surface, then stir in with a round-bladed knife until the dough sticks together and leaves the sides of the bowl cleanly.

2 Turn out on to a floured surface and knead lightly until firm and smooth. Wrap in cling film and leave to rest in the refrigerator for about 30 minutes.

3 Meanwhile, prepare the barbecue.

4 Divide the pastry into 10 portions and roll each one into a ball. Make a deep hollow in each one and fill with ½ teaspoon apricot conserve. Shape the pastry over the filling to enclose it, then gently flatten to about 2 cm/¾ inch thickness. Press a fork down on each side to make a decorative pattern.

5 When the charcoal has reached the white ash stage, arrange the pastries on the barbecue grill and cook well above the coals for 15 minutes, turning the pastries over halfway through. Dust with icing sugar and serve.

◆ Ideally, cook the pastries when the barbecue has been going for a while and is not so hot. It is essential to cook them at least 5-7.5 cm/2-3 inches above the coals or the outside will burn before they are cooked through.

Barbecued peaches

SAUCES

Sauces and relishes are used to add delicious flavours to
barbecued food. Some savoury sauces can be brushed on
kebabs and burgers before and during cooking. Sweet sauces
are delicious served warm with fruit kebabs.

Chilli sauce

Makes about 150 ml/¼ pint
2 tablespoons olive oil
1 onion, chopped
2 garlic cloves, crushed
½ teaspoon turmeric
1 teaspoon coriander seeds, crushed
1 teaspoon ground cumin
4 dried red chillies, crushed
2 tablespoons soy sauce
salt and freshly ground black pepper
300 ml/½ pint water

1 Heat the oil in a saucepan, add the onion and
fry gently for 5 minutes until soft. Stir in the garlic,
turmeric, coriander seeds, cumin and chillies and
fry for a further 1-2 minutes.
2 Add the soy sauce, seasoning and the water.
Bring to the boil and simmer for 5-10 minutes.
3 Allow to cool slightly, then purée in a blender or
food processor, then press through a sieve.
Reheat gently to serve.

◆ This makes a hot sauce for serving with
vegetable kebabs or Soya burgers (see page 22). If
a milder flavour is preferred, reduce the amount
of chillies, turmeric and cumin.

Italian walnut sauce

Serves 4
100 g/4 oz walnut pieces
1-2 tablespoons finely chopped fresh marjoram or parsley
125 ml/4 fl oz double cream
about 1 tablespoon olive oil
salt and freshly ground black pepper

1 Grind the walnuts to a paste in a coffee mill,
blender or food processor with the finely chopped
marjoram or parsley. Alternatively, mince the
nuts, then pound them to a paste with a pestle in
a mortar – the paste need not be completely
smooth.
2 Transfer the paste to a serving dish and slowly
mix in the cream, blending it in thoroughly. The
paste should be fairly soft and pale green in
colour.
3 Gradually stir in the olive oil, adding just enough
to make the sauce like a soft purée. Season to
taste with salt and freshly ground black pepper
and keep in the refrigerator until ready to serve.

◆ This famous, creamy, purée-like sauce is called
salsa di noci in Italy. It can be served with any
vegetable burgers, kebabs or stuffed vegetable. It
is also extremely tasty spooned over hot pasta,
particularly tagliatelle, with grated Parmesan
cheese sprinkled over the top. This amount of
sauce is enough for about 350 g/12 oz tagliatelle
or other pasta, and served like this makes an ideal
starter.

Barbecue sauce

Makes about 175 ml/6 fl oz

25 g/1 oz butter or margarine

1 onion, chopped

1 garlic clove, crushed

2 cm/¾ inch piece of root ginger, peeled and chopped

2 tablespoons red wine vinegar

150 ml/¼ pint water

1 teaspoon made English mustard

1 tablespoon dark muscovado sugar

2 tablespoons tomato purée

1 teaspoon soy sauce

salt and freshly ground black pepper

1 Melt the butter or margarine in a saucepan, add the onion, garlic and ginger and fry gently for 5 minutes or until soft.

2 Mix together the remaining ingredients, seasoning to taste with salt and pepper, and add to the onion mixture. Bring to the boil, stirring, then lower the heat and simmer, uncovered, for 10 minutes.

3 Remove from the heat and allow to cool slightly, then purée in a blender or food processor. Return the sauce to the rinsed out pan and reheat gently.

◆ This sauce can be used for brushing kebabs, Soya burgers (see page 22) or Garlicky aubergine slices (see page 26). Alternatively serve separately with Soya burgers or Cheesy potato cakes (see page 24).

Peanut baste

Serves 6

6 tablespoons smooth peanut butter

175 ml/6 fl oz orange juice

1 Put the peanut butter and orange juice in a small saucepan and heat gently until the consistency of a smooth paste.

2 Brush over any vegetable kebabs just before barbecuing and continue to baste the kebabs with the sauce during cooking.

Variation
◆ This is quite a sweet baste, for a spicier flavour add a small pinch of chilli powder before heating the peanut butter and orange juice.

Fresh tomato sauce

Makes about 300 ml/½ pint
500 g/1 lb tomatoes, chopped
5 cm/2 inch piece of cinnamon stick
1 blade of mace
150 ml/¼ pint water
1 teaspoon tarragon vinegar
1 tarragon sprig, chopped
½ teaspoon paprika
pinch of cayenne pepper
salt and freshly ground black pepper

1 Place the tomatoes in a heavy-based saucepan with the cinnamon, mace and water. Bring to the boil, then reduce the heat and simmer for 5 minutes. Discard the cinnamon.
2 Remove from the heat and allow to cool slightly, then purée in a blender or food processor. Press through a sieve to remove the seeds, then return the purée to the rinsed out pan. Add the remaining ingredients, seasoning to taste with salt and pepper.
3 Bring to the boil, then reduce the heat and boil for 5-10 minutes, stirring frequently, to slightly reduce the liquid and concentrate the flavour. Serve hot.

◆ Serve with vegetable kebabs, Soya burgers (see page 22) or Stuffed peppers or Rice-filled courgettes (see pages 14 and 18).

Mustard sauce

Makes about 300 ml/½ pint
25 g/1 oz butter
25 g/1 oz plain flour
150 ml/¼ pint vegetable stock
150 ml/¼ pint milk
1 teaspoon mustard powder
1 teaspoon white wine vinegar
salt and freshly ground black pepper

1 Melt the butter in a small saucepan, add the flour and cook for 1 minute.
2 Remove from the heat and gradually stir in the stock and milk. Return to the heat and bring to the boil, stirring.
3 Reduce heat, and stir in the mustard powder and vinegar and season to taste with salt and pepper. Serve hot.

◆ Serve the sauce with vegetable burgers or kebabs.

Fresh tomato sauce, served with barbecued vegetable kebabs

Sweetcorn relish

Serves 6-10

225 g/8 oz sweetcorn kernels, defrosted if frozen

½ green pepper, deseeded and chopped

½ red pepper, deseeded and chopped

3 celery stalks, chopped

1 onion, finely chopped

2.5 cm/1 inch piece of root ginger, peeled and finely chopped

1 teaspoon salt

1½ teaspoons mustard powder

2 tablespoons caster sugar

450 ml/¾ pint white wine vinegar

1 Heat the oven to 140C/275F/Gas 1 and warm the jars while making the relish.

2 Place the sweetcorn in a large saucepan with the peppers, celery, onion and ginger.

3 In a bowl, mix together the salt, mustard and sugar with a little of the vinegar, then stir in the rest of the vinegar.

4 Pour the vinegar over the vegetables in the pan and bring to the boil. Reduce the heat and simmer, uncovered, for 15-20 minutes, stirring frequently.

5 Pour the relish into the warmed jars and seal with vinegar-proof lids.

◆ This relish can be kept for up to a week.

Pepper relish

Serves 6-8

1 tablespoon olive oil

1 onion, chopped

½ teaspoon ground cumin

50 g/2 oz French beans, chopped

2 large green peppers, deseeded and chopped

2 large red peppers, deseeded and chopped

225 g/8 oz tomatoes, skinned and chopped

4 tablespoons white wine vinegar

1 Heat the oil in a saucepan, add the onion and fry gently for 5 minutes or until soft. Stir in the cumin and cook for 1 minute.

2 Meanwhile, cook the beans in boiling water for 1-2 minutes and blanch the peppers in boiling water for 30 seconds. Drain well.

3 Add the beans, peppers and tomatoes to the onion mixture and stir in the vinegar. Bring to the boil, then reduce the heat and simmer for 3-5 minutes until most of the liquid has evaporated.

4 Transfer to a serving bowl and leave until cold.

◆ This relish can be kept in the refrigerator for 4-5 days.

◆ Serve with kebabs or burgers. Alternatively, serve as a side salad. It will serve 4 people when served as a salad.

Chocolate sauce

Makes about 250 ml/8 fl oz

175 g/6 oz plain dessert chocolate, broken into pieces

40 g/1½ oz butter

50 g/2 oz light soft brown sugar

150 ml/¼ pint water

2-3 tablespoons Cointreau

1 Put the chocolate into a heavy-based saucepan with the butter, sugar and water.
2 Heat gently, stirring, until the chocolate, butter and sugar have dissolved. Bring to the boil, stir in the Cointreau and simmer, uncovered, for 5-10 minutes until thick.

Variation
◆ Cointreau gives the sauce a delicious orange flavour, but any liqueur of your choice can be used instead. Alternatively, the liqueur can be omitted if wished.

Rum fudge sauce

Makes about 150 ml/¼ pint

175 ml/6 fl oz double cream

50 g/2 oz unsalted butter

4 tablespoons soft brown sugar

1 tablespoon dark muscovado sugar

1 tablespoon rum

1 Place the cream and butter in a heavy-based saucepan and heat gently, stirring, until the butter has melted.
2 Bring to the boil, then stir in the brown sugars. Heat gently until dissolved, then stir in the rum, bring to the boil and boil for 2 minutes until thick.
3 Keep warm on the side of the barbecue until ready to serve.

◆ This delicious sauce can be served with fruit kebabs, baked apples or ice cream. In winter it can be served with steamed sponge puddings.

PICNICS

Picnics are fun, and keep down the cost of a family outing – a picnic meal costs far less than trying to feed a family of six at a restaurant or café, and few out of the way snack bars and cafés cater for vegetarians. A homemade picnic provides far more variety using wholesome fresh ingredients that will satisfy the heartiest appetite.

Picnic equipment

Nowadays there is an enormous range of picnic ware and its greatest advantage over old-fashioned hampers is that it is light and easy to carry. All the food in these recipes can be packed in rigid plastic containers unless otherwise stated. Some foods such as Falafel in pitta pockets (see page 52) may need wrapping in cling film or aluminium foil before being packed.

Insulated cool bags with chemical ice-packs placed inside them are perfect for keeping food beautifully cool until you are ready to eat it. Pop the ice-packs in the freezer or the freezing compartment of the refrigerator the night before, so that they freeze solid, then place them in the bottom of the insulated bag – they will remain frozen solid for several hours even on hot days.

A cold box with an ice-pack wedged in amongst the food will keep things cold for longer than an insulated bag, but cold boxes have the disadvantage of being quite heavy which is worth considering if you have to carry them for long distances.

Vacuum flasks will keep foods like soup or coffee piping hot, or cold foods well chilled. Use wide-necked flasks for solid foods and narrow-necked ones for hot or cold drinks.

Cling film and aluminium foil are invaluable for wrapping foods, and paper plates with matching napkins mean there's no washing up when you get home. Plastic mugs are good for tea and coffee or children's drinks, but wine tastes much nicer in a clear plastic tumbler.

Take a cloth to lay the food out on, a corkscrew and a bottle opener, a sharp knife and a stout plastic bag for rubbish.

Food for picnics

Picnic food needs to be easy to eat with only fingers or fork – very fiddly food is likely to be totally unappetising by the time it reaches the picnic site and has been unpacked and spread out ready for eating. The food in this chapter is either easy to pack in rigid container or can be transported in the dish in which it was cooked.

Foods in edible containers are even better. Mushroom brioches (see page 47) – individual brioches baked with a filling inside – or Brown lentil pasties (see page 43) are good examples. Remember also that people like to have as much filling as container when it comes to filling sandwiches.

Fruits other than apples are difficult to take on a picnic as they tend to get bruised and squashed on the journey, so here they have been used to make cakes and pastries such as Apple and ginger cake (see page 62), Fruit tartlets and Cherry and almond baklava (see page 66).

Salads have not been included in this chapter as any of the salads from pages 68-75 can be packed in rigid plastic containers and taken on a picnic. Transport the dressing in a small screw-topped jar or plastic container with a secure lid.

Brown lentil pasties

PIES

Pies are some of the easiest foods to take on a picnic and they
make a welcome change from endless sandwiches. Use
wholewheat flour for the pastry and try adding chopped nuts to
the dough for a crunchy texture (see page 43).
Try experimenting with different vegetables for fillings.

Provençal pie

Serves 6
2 tablespoons olive oil
350 g/12 oz mushrooms, sliced
225 g/8 oz courgettes, sliced
4 spring onions, sliced
1 tablespoon chopped fresh thyme
2 tablespoons plain flour
225 g/8 oz can chopped tomatoes
salt and freshly ground black pepper
PASTRY
275 g/10 oz plain flour
pinch of salt
150 g/5 oz margarine or butter, diced
about 5 tablespoons water
beaten egg, to glaze

1 Heat the oil in a large saucepan, add the
mushrooms, courgettes, spring onions and
thyme and cook gently for 5 minutes. Stir in the
flour, then the tomatoes and cook, stirring occasionally, until thickened. Season to taste with salt
and pepper and leave to cool.
2 Heat the oven to 200C/400F/Gas 6.
3 Make the pastry: sift the flour and salt into a
bowl. Add the margarine or butter and rub into
the flour until the mixture resembles fine breadcrumbs. Mix in just enough water to make a soft
elastic dough. Wrap the dough in cling film and
refrigerate for 30 minutes.
4 Remove one-third of the dough and roll out on
a floured surface to a 23 cm/9 inch round; set
aside. Roll out the remaining pastry and use to
line a 20 cm/8 inch flan ring or pie dish. Spoon the
filling into the pastry case.
5 Dampen the edge of the pastry and place the
reserved round of pastry on top. Press the edges
together to seal, trim away the excess pastry and
crimp the edges neatly.
6 Re-roll the trimmings and cut out 6 leaf shapes.
Brush the top of the pie with beaten egg, stick the
leaves on top and brush the leaves with egg. Cut
a hole in the centre for the steam to escape and
bake for 40-50 minutes until the pastry is golden
brown.

◆ When using a glass or ceramic pie dish for a
double crust pie, place a baking sheet in the oven
to heat. Place the pie dish on the heated baking
sheet – the extra initial heat helps ensure that the
base cooks through.

Variation
◆ For a pie with an even heartier flavour use
sliced leeks instead of the courgettes.

Brown lentil pasties

Makes 6

100 g/4 oz brown lentils

4 carrots, diced

1 onion, finely chopped

100 g/4 oz cooked peas

1 tablespoon tomato purée

1 tablespoon chopped fresh parsley

salt and freshly ground black pepper

beaten egg, to glaze

PASTRY

400 g/14 oz wholewheat flour

pinch of salt

200 g/7 oz margarine or butter, diced

about 6 tablespoons water

1 Heat the oven to 200C/400F/Gas 6.
2 Make the pastry: sift the flour and salt into a bowl. Add the margarine or butter and rub into the flour with your fingertips until the mixture resembles fine breadcrumbs. Mix in just enough water to make a soft elastic dough. Wrap the dough in cling film and refrigerate for 30 minutes.
3 Meanwhile, make the filling: cook the lentils in boiling salted water for 15-20 minutes until tender, then drain and leave to cool.
4 Cook the carrots in boiling salted water for 5 minutes until tender, then drain and leave to cool.
5 Mix together the lentils, carrots, onion, peas, tomato purée, parsley and salt and pepper to taste.
6 Divide the dough into 6 pieces and roll out each piece on a floured surface to a 15 cm/6 inch round.
7 Put a portion of the filling on the centre of each round. Brush water halfway around the edge of each. Press the sides together over the filling to seal. Crimp the edges neatly and brush all over with beaten egg.
8 Put the pasties on a baking sheet and bake for 15 minutes. Reduce the heat to 180C/350F/Gas 4 and bake for a further 30-40 minutes until well browned. Leave to cool on a wire rack.

Variation
◆ Substitute 100 g/4 oz canned sweetcorn kernels for the peas, if preferred.

Crunchy nut Cheshire flan

Serves 6

2 onions, chopped

225 g/8 oz red Cheshire cheese, grated

2 eggs, beaten

salt and freshly ground black pepper

3 tomatoes, sliced

PASTRY

100 g/4 oz wholewheat flour

pinch of salt

50 g/2 oz finely chopped nuts

75 g/3 oz margarine or butter, diced

about 3 tablespoons water

1 Heat the oven to 200C/400F/Gas 6.
2 Make the pastry: sift the flour and salt into a bowl, add the nuts and margarine or butter. Rub in the margarine until the mixture resembles fine breadcrumbs. Mix in just enough water to make a soft elastic dough. Wrap the dough in cling film and refrigerate for 30 minutes.
3 Place the onions in a small saucepan and cover with boiling water. Bring back to the boil and simmer for 5 minutes. Drain and leave to cool.
4 Roll out the pastry on a floured surface and use to line a 20 cm/8 inch flan dish. Prick the base with a fork and place a large circle of greaseproof paper in the pastry case; weight it down with baking beans.
5 Bake the pastry case for 15 minutes. Remove paper and beans and bake 5 minutes more.
6 Reserve 15 g/½ oz of the cheese and stir the remainder into the onions with the eggs and salt and pepper to taste. Spoon into the pastry case and smooth the surface. Arrange the tomato slices in an overlapping circle around the edge and sprinkle with the reserved cheese.
7 Bake in the oven for 15 minutes, then reduce the temperature to 180C/350F/Gas 4 for a further 15 minutes or until filling is set and golden.

Variations
◆ Cheddar, Double Gloucester or Red Leicester are all suitable for this flan.

◆ Stir 2 tablespoons chopped fresh parsley, thyme or chives, into the mixture with the eggs.

Asparagus flan

Serves 6

350 g/12 oz fresh asparagus

2 eggs

150 ml/¼ pint milk

50 ml/2 fl oz double cream

1 tablespoon chopped fresh dill

salt and freshly ground black pepper

dill sprigs, to garnish

PASTRY

175 g/6 oz wholewheat flour

pinch of salt

75 g/3 oz margarine or butter, diced

about 3 tablespoons water

1 Heat the oven to 200C/400F/Gas 6.

2 Make the pastry: sift the flour and salt into a bowl. Add the margarine or butter and rub into the flour with your fingertips until the mixture resembles fine breadcrumbs. Mix in just enough water to make a soft elastic dough. Wrap the dough in cling film and refrigerate for 30 minutes.

3 Make the filling: cook the asparagus in a large saucepan of boiling salted water for 5-7 minutes until just tender. Rinse under cold running water, then drain.

4 Cut a 7.5cm/3 inch 'tip' from each asparagus spear, then chop the remainder of the spears into 1 cm/½ inch lengths and set aside.

5 In a bowl, whisk together the eggs, milk, cream, dill and salt and pepper to taste.

6 Roll out the pastry on a floured surface and use to line a 20 cm/8 inch flan dish. Prick the base with a fork and place a large circle of greaseproof paper in the pastry case; weight it down with baking beans.

7 Bake the pastry case for 15 minutes. Remove the paper and the beans and bake 5 minutes more.

8 Scatter chopped asparagus over the base of the pastry case, pour in the egg mixture. Top with asparagus tips in a pinwheel design.

9 Reduce the heat to 180C/350F/Gas 4 and bake the flan for about 35 minutes until set and golden. Garnish with sprigs of dill.

◆ To give pastry a crisp finish brush inside of case with beaten egg after removing baking beans.

Asparagus flan

Tomato and aubergine samosas

Makes 15

3 tablespoons vegetable oil

1 large onion, chopped

3 carrots, diced

225 g/8 oz aubergine, diced

½ teaspoon ground allspice

½ teaspoon chilli powder

4 tomatoes, skinned and chopped

2 tablespoons chopped fresh mint

salt and freshly ground black pepper

375 g/13 oz packet puff pastry

vegetable oil, for deep frying

1 Heat the oil in a saucepan, add the onion and carrots and cook gently for 5 minutes until soft. Add the aubergine, allspice and chilli powder and cook for a further 5 minutes, stirring occasionally.
2 Remove pan from the heat. Stir in tomatoes mint and salt and pepper to taste. Leave to cool.
3 Roll out the pastry on a floured surface to a 30 × 50.5 cm/12 × 20 inch rectangle. Cut into 15 squares about 10 cm/4 inches each.
4 Divide the filling between the squares, brush the edges of the pastry with water and bring over one corner to form a triangle. Press the edges together to seal and crimp the edges neatly.
5 Heat the oil in a deep-fat frier with a basket to 180C/350F or until a day-old bread cube browns in 60 seconds. Put 3 samosas into the basket, then lower into the oil and cook for 4-5 minutes until the pastry turns golden. Drain on absorbent paper while frying the remaining samosas in the same way. Leave to cool before packing in a rigid container. The samosas can also be served warm.

◆ The samosas can be frozen for up to 3 months before frying. Open freeze until solid, then pack, separating them with freezer tissue. Deep-fry from frozen for about 6-8 minutes.

Variation
◆ Use up left-over cooked vegetables such as potato, peas or carrots to make different fillings – cook the onion with the spices until soft, then add about 350 g/12 oz cooked diced vegetables with the mint and seasoning.

Pizza scones

Makes 10

100 g/4 oz wholewheat self-raising flour

100 g/4 oz white self-raising flour

½ teaspoon salt

50 g/2 oz margarine or butter, diced

2 tablespoons chopped fresh parsley and thyme mixed

125 ml/4 fl oz milk

vegetable oil, for greasing

TOPPING

2 tablespoons olive oil

6 spring onions, chopped

7 tomatoes, skinned and chopped

3 tablespoons tomato purée

1 teaspoon chopped fresh thyme

salt and freshly ground black pepper

75 g/3 oz Mozzarella cheese, grated

6 pimiento-stuffed olives, sliced

1 Heat the oven to 220C/425F/Gas 7. Grease a baking sheet.
2 Sift the flours and salt into a bowl. Add the margarine or butter and rub into the flour until the mixture resembles fine breadcrumbs. Add the herbs and mix to a soft dough with the milk.
3 Knead the dough lightly, then roll out on a floured surface and cut out 10 rounds using a 10 cm/4 inch plain round cutter. Place on the baking sheet.
4 Make the topping: heat the oil in a saucepan, add the onions, tomatoes, tomato purée, thyme and salt and pepper to taste. Bring to the boil, then simmer uncovered for 3-5 minutes until thickened.
5 Spread a portion of the topping on each scone round. Sprinkle with the cheese and olives and bake for 15-20 minutes until the scone is well risen and the cheese golden brown and bubbling. Transfer to a wire rack to cool.

◆ When making the scones you can use 225 g/8 oz 81% wholewheat self-raising flour in place of the wholewheat and white self-raising flour mixture if preferred.

ALL-IN-ONE FOOD

The recipes in this section are the equivalent of main courses and need only bread or a salad to accompany them. They include a vegetarian version of Scotch eggs, Stuffed vine leaves and a terrine made from beans that can be transported in the tin it is made in.

Mushroom brioches

Makes 16

500 g/1 lb strong white flour

1 teaspoon salt

2 teaspoons easy-blend dried yeast

25 g/1 oz caster sugar

4 eggs, beaten

175 g/6 oz butter, melted

6 tablespoons hand-hot water

beaten egg, to glaze

FILLING

25 g/1 oz butter

175 g/6 oz mushrooms, finely chopped

salt and freshly ground black pepper

1 Grease 16 small brioche tins or 16 tartlet tins.
2 Sift the flour and salt into a large bowl. Stir in the yeast and sugar until well mixed. Make a well in the centre and pour in the eggs, butter and water. Beat with one hand for about 10 minutes to form a fairly soft, glossy dough.
3 Cover the bowl tightly with cling film and leave to rise in a warm place for an hour.
4 Meanwhile, make the filling: melt the butter in a saucepan, add the mushrooms and cook over a medium heat for 3-4 minutes until softened. Remove from the heat before the mushrooms begin to sweat. Season and set aside.
5 Turn the dough out on to a floured surface and knead lightly. Cut off one-third of the dough and set aside covered with cling film. Cut the remaining dough into 16 pieces, roll each out to a 6.5 cm/2½ inch circle and use to line the brioche tins.
6 Divide the filling between the tins. Cut the remaining dough into 16 pieces, roll into balls and flatten slightly. Brush the base of the balls with egg glaze and press one on to each of the lined tins, completely enclosing the filling.
7 Cover with a dry tea towel and leave to prove in a warm place for about 40 minutes, or until doubled in size.
8 About 20 minutes before the dough is ready for baking, heat the oven to 230C/450F/Gas 8.
9 Uncover the brioches and brush with beaten egg. Bake in the oven for about 10 minutes until risen and golden brown. Remove from the tins and cool on a wire rack. Pack in polythene bags.

◆ The initial mixing and kneading of the dough can be done in a food processor. Fit a plastic dough blade and place the flour, salt, yeast and sugar in the bowl of the processor. Switch on, pour the eggs, butter and water through the feed tube and process for 3-4 minutes until dough is smooth and glossy. Transfer to oiled bowl to rise.

◆ Make sure that the balls of dough are sealed all the way round with egg glaze so that the brioches keep their shape during baking.

◆ These brioches are also delicious served warm if eaten at home.

Stuffed vine leaves

Serves 4-6

225 g/8 oz packet vine leaves in brine

75 g/3 oz split red lentils

50 g/2 oz bulgar wheat

1 tablespoon olive oil

½ onion, finely chopped

25 g/1 oz sultanas

6 prunes, soaked overnight, then stoned and chopped

1 teaspoon chopped fresh mint or ½ teaspoon dried

½ teaspoon ground cinnamon

salt and freshly ground black pepper

1 Rinse the vine leaves, then cover with boiling water and leave to soak for 20 minutes. Drain, then soak in cold water for a further 20 minutes. Drain well and pat dry with absorbent paper.

2 While the leaves are soaking, place the lentils in a saucepan, cover with cold water and bring to the boil. Reduce the heat and simmer for 5 minutes; drain and set aside.

3 Put the bulgar wheat in a small bowl, cover with 150 ml/¼ pint boiling water and leave to soak for 15 minutes. Drain the wheat in a sieve and, using your hands, squeeze out as much water as possible.

4 Heat the oil in a pan, add the onion and cook for 5 minutes until soft. Remove from the heat and add the lentils, bulgar wheat, sultanas, prunes, mint, cinnamon and salt and pepper to taste.

5 To stuff the vine leaves: place a heaped spoonful of the filling mixture in the centre of the veined side of each leaf, then fold over the stalk end to cover the filling. Fold in both sides of the leaf towards the middle so that the filling is completely enclosed, then roll up from the stalk end to form a tight, neat roll.

6 Place the stuffed vine leaves, seam side downwards, in the base of a small pan. Cover with salted water and place a saucer on top of the vine leaves to hold them securely in place. Bring to the boil, then reduce the heat and simmer gently for 50 minutes. Leave the vine leaves to cool in the cooking liquid, then drain.

Vegetarian Scotch eggs

Makes 4

4 eggs

400 g/14 oz can butter beans, drained

100 g/4 oz Cheddar cheese, grated

3 tablespoons crunchy peanut butter

salt and freshly ground black pepper

TO COAT

25 g/1 oz toasted breadcrumbs

1 tablespoon chopped fresh parsley

1 Place the eggs in a small saucepan and cover with cold water. Bring to the boil, then reduce the heat and simmer gently for 10 minutes. Drain, cool under cold running water and remove the shells. Dry the eggs with absorbent paper.

2 Mash the beans in a bowl until smooth. Add the cheese, peanut butter and salt and pepper to taste and beat until well blended.

3 Divide the cheese mixture into 4 portions. Press each piece out to a 2 cm/¾ inch thick oval on a sheet of cling film. With damp hands, mould the cheese mixture round the eggs to completely cover.

4 Mix together the breadcrumbs and parsley and roll the Scotch eggs in the mixture to coat.

◆ Eggs continue cooking in their own heat and if not cooled quickly in cold water a dark ring may form round the yolk.

Variation
◆ Use 25 g/1 oz chopped toasted nuts to replace half of the breadcrumbs for the coating.

Vegetarian Scotch eggs

Bean terrine

Serves 6

1 kg/2 lb fresh or frozen broad beans

1 courgette, sliced

50 g/2 oz French beans

4 carrots

4 eggs

4 tablespoons double cream

1 tablespoon chopped fresh parsley

salt and freshly ground black pepper

2 canned pimientos

vegetable oil, for greasing

1 Heat the oven to 170C/325F/Gas 3. Grease an 850 g/1¾ lb, 1.5 L/2½ pint capacity, loaf tin. Line base and sides with greased greaseproof paper.
2 Cook the broad beans, courgette, French beans and carrots separately in boiling salted water until tender. Rinse under cold running water, drain and set aside.
3 Purée the broad beans in a blender or food processor until smooth, then beat in the eggs, cream, parsley and salt and pepper to taste.
4 Arrange the sliced courgette in the base of the tin and spoon one-quarter of the broad bean mixture over them.
5 Cut the pimientos in half and arrange over the broad bean mixture. Spoon over another quarter of the mixture.
6 Lay the French beans lengthways on top and spoon over a further quarter of the mixture.
7 Arrange the whole carrots lengthways on top and cover with the remaining broad bean mixture. Cover the loaf tin with greased greaseproof paper, place in a roasting tin half-full of boiling water and bake for 1 hour, or until set.
8 Remove the tin from the water and leave until cold. Turn the loaf out, remove the lining paper and serve in thick slices.

◆ Choose very long thin carrots – or use 8 smaller carrots.

◆ When transporting the terrine to a picnic, either leave in the loaf tin and cover tightly with cling film, or turn out, slice and interleave with freezer tissue or cling film and pack in a rigid container.

Picnic vol-au-vents

Makes 16

16 frozen vol-au-vents, each about 4.5 cm/1¾ inches in diameter

beaten egg, to glaze

FILLING

25 g/1 oz margarine or butter

225 g/8 oz tiny button mushrooms

2 teaspoons lemon juice

25 g/1 oz plain flour

300 ml/½ pint milk

2 tablespoons double cream

2 tablespoons chopped fresh chives

salt and freshly ground black pepper

freshly grated nutmeg

1 Heat the oven to 220C/425F/Gas 7. Dampen a large baking sheet.
2 Brush the rims of the frozen vol-au-vents with beaten egg and place about 1 cm/½ inch apart on the baking sheet. Bake in the oven for about 15 minutes until golden and well risen. Transfer to a wire rack to cool.
3 Heat the margarine or butter in a saucepan, add the mushrooms and lemon juice and cook over a medium heat for 2 minutes. Stir in the flour, then gradually add the milk. Bring to the boil stirring constantly until smooth and thickened. Simmer for 2 minutes, then stir in the cream, chives and salt, pepper and nutmeg to taste. Leave to cool. To prevent a skin forming on the sauce as it cools, cover the surface with cling film.
4 Remove the lids from the vol-au-vents, spoon the mushroom sauce into the middle and replace the lids. The vol-au-vents are best kept cool and eaten the day of making.

Variation
◆ Omit the mushrooms, chives and nutmeg and add a 200 g/7 oz can sweetcorn kernels, 2 deseeded and chopped tomatoes and 2 tablespoons chopped fresh parsley.

Potted cheese

Makes 350 g/12 oz

100 g/4 oz butter, diced

225 g/8 oz Gruyère cheese, finely grated

2 tablespoons milk

salt and freshly ground black pepper

freshly grated nutmeg

1 Place the butter in a bowl, beat until soft, then gradually beat in the cheese and milk. Season to taste with salt, pepper and nutmeg.

2 Transfer to a jar or plastic container to transport. Serve spread on crackers or crispbread or use as a sandwich filling.

◆ The flavour is improved if the cheese is made the day before and refrigerated overnight to allow the flavour to mature.

Variation

◆ For a special-occasion potted cheese, add 100g /4 oz chopped stoned cherries and substitute 1 tablespoon kirsch for half of the milk. Beat in the chopped cherries until the cheese is pink.

Herby egg Charlottes

Makes 4

75 g/3 oz margarine or butter

15 g/½ oz plain flour

150 ml/¼ pint milk

3 hard-boiled eggs, chopped

2 tablespoons chopped mixed fresh herbs

salt and freshly ground black pepper

8 large slices wholewheat bread

1 Heat the oven to 190C/375F/Gas 5.

2 Melt 15 g/½ oz of the margarine or butter in a saucepan, add the flour and cook for a minute. Gradually stir in the milk and cook until thickened and smooth. Stir in the eggs, herbs and salt and pepper to taste.

3 Melt the remaining margarine or butter. Cut the crusts from the bread, dip 4 of the slices in the melted margarine or butter and use to line 4 ramekin dishes, trimming to fit.

4 Spoon the egg sauce into the bread-lined ramekins. Cut the remaining bread into circles to fit inside the ramekins, dip in the margarine or butter and press on top of the filling.

5 Bake the Charlottes in the oven for 25-30 minutes until crisp and golden. Leave to cool for a few minutes then turn out on to a wire rack to cool.

◆ The Charlottes are also delicious served hot as a starter.

Cheese, courgette and cashew rissoles

Makes 16

175 g/6 oz Red Leicester cheese, finely grated

150 g/5 oz cream cheese

75 g/3 oz butter, diced

1 courgette, finely grated

100 g/4 oz cashew nuts, chopped

few drops of Tabasco sauce

salt

40 g/1½ oz toasted breadcrumbs, for coating

1 Place the cheeses, butter, courgette and nuts in a bowl. Add the Tabasco and salt to taste. Beat until well blended.

2 Divide into 16 pieces then, using damp hands, form into rissole shapes. Roll in breadcrumbs to coat completely.

◆ The rissoles can be frozen for up to 3 months. Open freeze until solid, then pack in a rigid container, separating the layers with freezer tissue. To serve, uncover and defrost for 4 hours at room temperature.

Variation

◆ Instead of plain cream cheese, use a flavoured cream cheese such as garlic and herb.

Falafel in pitta pockets

Serves 6

2 × 400 g/14 oz cans chick peas, drained

1 onion, finely chopped

1 garlic clove, crushed

1 teaspoon ground cumin

1 teaspoon ground coriander

1 tablespoon chopped fresh parsley or coriander

1 tablespoon olive oil

50 g/2 oz fresh wholemeal breadcrumbs

25 g/1 oz wholewheat flour, for dusting

vegetable oil, for frying

3 round pitta breads, about 15 cm/6 inches in diameter

CARAWAY COLESLAW

175 g/6 oz cabbage, finely shredded

½ small onion, finely sliced

2 carrots, grated

1 tablespoon chopped fresh chives

3 tablespoons mayonnaise

½ teaspoon caraway seeds

salt and freshly ground black pepper

1 Place the chick peas in a bowl and mash until smooth. Stir in the onion, garlic, cumin, coriander, parsley, oil and breadcrumbs and mix to a firm paste. Form the mixture into 24 balls and flatten them slightly. Dust with flour.

2 Heat a little oil in a frying pan and fry the falafel in batches until golden brown, turning once. Drain on absorbent paper and leave to cool.

3 To make the coleslaw: place all the ingredients in a bowl and toss until the cabbage is well coated in mayonnaise.

4 Halve pitta breads and ease open to form pockets. Fill each with 4 falafel and some coleslaw.

◆ The chick peas can be puréed in a food processor, but do not overprocess them.

◆ Wrap the pitta pockets individually in cling film and pack into polythene bags. Alternatively, pack the pitta bread, coleslaw and falafel separately for transporting to the picnic site.

Falafel in pitta pockets

SANDWICHES

Sandwiches are traditional picnic fare, but making your own,
unusual breads turns them into an imaginative meal.
And everyone will love the savoury spreads using vegetables
like courgettes, carrots, cabbage, onion and cucumber, and
for the children there fun ideas like a Submarine sandwich.

Cheese and onion bread

Makes 10-12 slices

225 g/8 oz 81% wholewheat flour

½ teaspoon salt

50 g/2 oz margarine or butter, diced

1 teaspoon sugar

1 teaspoon easy-blend dried yeast

150 ml/¼ pint warm milk

75 g/3 oz Cheddar cheese, grated

1 small onion, sliced into thin rings

beaten egg, to glaze

vegetable oil, for greasing

1 Grease an 8 × 15 cm/3½ × 6 inch loaf tin.
2 Sift the flour and salt into a large bowl. Add the margarine or butter and rub into the flour. Stir in the sugar and yeast, then make a well in the centre. Pour in the milk and mix to a dough.
3 Knead the dough on a floured surface for about 10 minutes, or until it is smooth and elastic. Place the dough in a large oiled bowl, cover tightly with cling film and leave to rise in a warm place for about an hour, or until the dough has doubled in size.

4 Turn the dough out on to a floured surface and knead lightly. Roll out to a 15 × 45 cm/6 × 18 inch rectangle. Reserve 15 g/½ oz of the cheese and 4 onion rings. Sprinkle the remainder evenly over the dough. Roll up tightly from a narrow end and place in the tin seam side down.
5 Cover the tin with oiled cling film and leave to prove in a warm place for about 40 minutes, or until doubled in size again.
6 About 20 minutes before the dough is ready for baking, heat the oven to 220C/425F/Gas 7.
7 Uncover the dough and brush with beaten egg. Arrange the reserved onion rings on top and bake in the oven for 30-40 minutes until risen and golden brown. About 10 minutes before the end of cooking, sprinkle the reserved cheese over the top. When cooked, turn out of the tin and cool on a wire rack.

◆ 81% wholewheat flour contains less bran and so gives a lighter effect than 100% wholewheat flour.

Variation
◆ Any type of cheese can be used – try Danish Blue, Double Gloucester with chives, Gruyére or Red Leicester.

Olive and thyme bread

Makes 8 pieces

225 g/8 oz wholewheat flour

225 g/8 oz strong white flour

2 teaspoons salt

75 g/3 oz margarine or butter, diced

1 teaspoon sugar

2 teaspoons easy-blend dried yeast

2 tablespoons chopped fresh thyme

50 g/2 oz pitted black olives, chopped

50 g/2 oz green pimiento-stuffed olives, chopped

250 ml/8 fl oz hand-hot water

beaten egg, to glaze

vegetable oil, for greasing

7 black olives, pitted, to garnish

1 Grease a deep 20 cm/8 inch round cake tin.
2 Sift the flours and salt into a large bowl. Add the margarine or butter and rub into the flours. Add the sugar, yeast, thyme and chopped olives and stir well. Make a well in the centre, pour in the water and mix to a dough.
3 Knead the dough on a floured surface for about 10 minutes, or until it is smooth and elastic. Place the dough in a large oiled bowl, cover tightly with cling film and leave in a warm place for about an hour until the dough has doubled in size.
4 Turn the dough out on to a floured surface and knead lightly. Cut into 8 even-sized pieces and roll each into a ball. Place one ball in the centre of the tin and arrange the remaining balls around it. Cover the tin with oiled cling film and leave to prove in a warm place for a further hour, or until the dough has doubled in size again.
5 About 20 minutes before the dough is ready for baking, heat the oven to 220C/425F/Gas 7.
6 Uncover the dough and brush with beaten egg. Press the whole olives in a ring around the centre ball of dough. Bake in the oven for 30-35 minutes until risen and golden brown. Turn out of the tin and cool on a wire rack.

◆ After sifting wholewheat flour, tip any bran caught in the sieve back into the bowl.

◆ When cool, the bread can be broken into 8 rolls for serving – there's no need for a bread knife!

Alfalfa bread

Makes 12-15 slices

500 g/1 lb strong white flour

1 teaspoon salt

75 g/3 oz white vegetable fat

2 teaspoons easy-blend dried yeast

300 ml/½ pint hand-hot water

75 g/3 oz alfalfa sprouts

2 tablespoons chopped fresh parsley

beaten egg, to glaze

vegetable oil, for greasing

1 Grease a 10 × 23 cm/4 × 9 inch loaf tin.
2 Sift the flour and salt into a large bowl. Add the fat and rub into the flour. Stir in the yeast and make a well in the centre. Pour in the water and mix to a dough.
3 Knead the dough on a floured surface for about 10 minutes, or until it is smooth and elastic, then knead in the alfalfa sprouts and parsley. Place the dough in a large oiled bowl, cover tightly and leave to rise in a warm place for about an hour, or until the dough has doubled in size.
4 Turn the dough out on to a floured surface and knead lightly. Pat the dough out to a 23 cm/9 inch square and roll up neatly. Place the rolled dough, seam side down, in the tin. Make 4 or 5 deep v-shaped snips in the surface with a large pair of scissors.
5 Cover the tin with oiled cling film and leave to prove in a warm place for about 1 hour, or until doubled in size again.
6 About 20 minutes before the dough is ready for baking, heat the oven to 220C/425F/Gas 7.
7 Uncover the dough and carefully brush with beaten egg. Bake in the oven for 40-50 minutes until risen and golden brown. Turn out of the tin and leave to cool on a wire rack.

◆ To test that the bread is done, turn it out of the tin and rap the underside smartly with your knuckles – it should sound hollow. If not, return the bread on its side to the oven and bake for a few minutes longer.

Surprise salad rolls

Makes 6

50 g/2 oz mushrooms, sliced

2 tomatoes, chopped

½ punnet salad cress

1 carrot, shredded

5 cm/2 inch piece cucumber, diced

100 g/4 oz Feta cheese, diced

2 tablespoons French dressing

6 crusty wholewheat rolls

margarine or butter, for spreading

1 Place the mushrooms, tomatoes, salad cress, carrot, cucumber and cheese in a bowl. Add the French dressing and toss to coat.

2 Cut the tops from the rolls and reserve. Carefully pull out the soft bread from inside each of the bases to leave 6 mm/¼ inch thick cases. Spread the inside of the cases and tops with margarine or butter.

3 Divide the salad filling between the cases and cover with the tops. Wrap the rolls individually in cling film, then pack in a polythene bag.

◆ Use the insides of the rolls to make bread-crumbs – pack them into a freezer bag and freeze for up to 3 months. Defrost at room temperature for 1 hour before using.

◆ For a decorative serving idea, cut the roll tops in half and arrange as butterfly wings.

Submarine sandwich

Serves 3-4

1 large French loaf

butter, for spreading

100 g/4 oz Edam cheese, sliced

8 small crisp lettuce leaves

3 tablespoons mayonnaise

2 tomatoes, sliced

5 cm/2 inch piece cucumber, sliced

salt and freshly ground black pepper

1 Cut the loaf in half horizontally. Spread the cut surfaces with butter. Arrange the cheese over the bottom half and top with lettuce.

2 Spoon the mayonnaise over the lettuce and cover with the tomatoes and cucumber slices. Season to taste with salt and pepper.

3 Place the top of the loaf over the filling. Cut the loaf diagonally into 8 pieces and wrap 2 pieces at a time tightly in cling film.

◆ Make the sandwich up to 3 hours in advance. To prevent the bottom half of the bread becoming soggy, make sure soft or wet ingredients are not touching the bread.

Variations

◆ Use sliced hard-boiled eggs, sliced soft cheeses such as Brie or Camembert, cottage cheese, hard cheeses or vegetable pâté to replace the Edam cheese.

◆ Add thinly sliced onion, salad cress, grated carrot, chicory or watercress.

◆ Omit the butter and spread both halves of the sandwich with a sandwich spread or flavoured cream cheese before filling with salad ingredients.

Surprise salad rolls

Vegetable sandwich spread

Makes about 750 g/1½ lb

175 g/6 oz white cabbage

¼ cucumber

½ onion, finely chopped

½ red pepper, deseeded and finely chopped

2 tablespoons chopped fresh chives

150 ml/¼ pint mayonnaise

175 g/6 oz cream cheese

2 teaspoons horseradish sauce

salt and freshly ground black pepper

1 Grate the cabbage into a bowl. Cut the cucumber into quarters lengthways and remove the seeds. Chop finely and add to the cabbage with the onion, red pepper and chives.

2 Mix together the mayonnaise, cream cheese, horseradish sauce and salt and pepper to taste. Stir into the vegetables until well mixed. Cover with cling film and refrigerate until ready to use.

Variations

◆ Replace 50 g/2 oz of the cabbage with finely chopped carrot or celery.

◆ Add up to 50 g/2 oz chopped walnuts or pecan nuts.

◆ Use other fresh herbs such as parsley or thyme.

Cheesy courgette and carrot spread

Makes about 500 g/1 lb

100 g/4 oz courgettes

100 g/4 oz carrots

100 g/4 oz Cheddar cheese

3 tablespoons mayonnaise

175 g/6 oz curd cheese

salt and cayenne pepper

1 Finely grate the courgettes, carrots and Cheddar cheese into a bowl.

2 Beat the mayonnaise into the curd cheese, then stir into the courgette mixture.

3 Season to taste with salt and cayenne pepper, cover with cling film and refrigerate spread until required.

◆ Make the spread up to 3 days in advance. Leave for 2 hours to soften before spreading.

Variation

◆ For a crunchy spread, add 75 g/3 oz chopped peanuts, cashew nuts or toasted sunflower seeds.

Aubergine and chick pea spread

Makes 500 g/1 lb

1 aubergine, about 225 g/8 oz

425 g/15 oz can chick peas, drained

1 garlic clove, crushed

4 tablespoons crunchy peanut butter

few drops of Tabasco sauce

2 teaspoons lemon juice

salt and freshly ground black pepper

1 Heat the oven to 190C/375F/Gas 5.
2 Prick the aubergine with a fork and bake in the oven for about 30 minutes or until soft. Leave to cool.
3 Purée the chick peas in a blender or food processor. Cut the aubergine in half and scoop out the flesh. Add to the chick pea purée with the garlic, peanut butter, Tabasco sauce, lemon juice and salt and pepper to taste. Work to a purée.

◆ Be careful not to over process the spread or it will become too thin.

◆ This sandwich spread can also be served as a dip with crisps and crudités.

Fruity-slaw baps

Makes 4

50 g/2 oz red cabbage

1 dessert apple

1 orange

25 g/1 oz sultanas

50 g/2 oz salted peanuts, chopped

25 g/1 oz beansprouts

2 tablespoons chopped fresh parsley

3 tablespoons mayonnaise

salt and freshly ground black pepper

4 large wholewheat baps

margarine or butter, for spreading

1 Finely shred the cabbage and core and coarsely grate the apple. Place in a bowl. Peel all the skin and pith from the orange and cut the segments from the membrane.
2 Squeeze any juice from the membrane over the cabbage and apple, then chop the orange segments and add to the bowl with the sultanas, peanuts, beansprouts, parsley, mayonnaise and salt and pepper to taste. Toss to coat.
3 Cut the baps in half horizontally and spread the cut surfaces with margarine or butter. Divide the mixture equally between the bap bases and cover with the tops.
4 Wrap the baps individually in cling film, then pack in a polythene bag.

◆ The fruity-slaw can be served on its own as a salad if wished.

Variation
◆ Any number of different ingredients can be used for this sandwich filling – substitute green, white or savoy cabbage, Chinese leaves, chopped grapefruit, avocado, raisins, sunflower seeds, cashew nuts, walnuts or chives.

SWEET TREATS

Finding suitable desserts for a picnic tends to be difficult:
delicate mousses are likely to collapse on the way, and many
other desserts will melt before they can be eaten.
The recipes here are made to be transported and will emerge
at the picnic looking none the worse for the journey.

Picnic cup cakes

Makes 18

100 g/4 oz margarine or butter, softened

100 g/4 oz caster sugar

2 eggs

100 g/4 oz self-raising flour

75 g/3 oz glacé cherries, chopped

ICING AND DECORATION

225 g/8 oz icing sugar

2-3 tablespoons warm water

9 glacé cherries, halved

1 Heat the oven to 180C/350F/Gas 4. Place 18 double cake cases on a baking sheet.
2 Place the margarine or butter and sugar in a bowl and beat until light and fluffy. Beat in the eggs a little at a time, beating well after each addition. Sift the flour and fold into the creamed mixture with the cherries.
3 Divide the mixture equally between the paper cases and smooth the surfaces. Bake in the oven for 15-20 minutes until golden brown and springy to the touch.
4 Transfer the cakes in their cases to a wire rack to cool.

5 Make the icing: sift the icing sugar into a bowl, then stir in just enough water to give a smooth coating consistency.
6 Spoon a little icing on top of each cake. Place a cherry half in the centre of each while the icing is still soft, then leave to set. Pack in a single layer in a rigid container.

◆ Store the cakes for up to 3 days in an airtight container. Or pack in freezer bags and freeze without the icing for up to 3 months. Defrost for 3-4 hours at room temperature, then unwrap and ice and decorate.

Variations
◆ Instead of cherries, use chopped almonds, walnuts or pecan nuts. Colour the icing with a few drops of food colouring, if wished, and top each cake with half a nut.

◆ To make chocolate cup cakes, substitute 65 g/2½ oz chocolate chips and 15 g/½ oz grated chocolate for the glacé cherries in the cake mixture. To flavour the icing, sift 4 teaspoons cocoa powder with the icing sugar before adding the water. After icing, top each cake with 2 or 3 chocolate chips.

Picnic cup cakes

Apricot teabread

Makes about 15 slices

100 g/4 oz wholewheat flour

100 g/4 oz plain flour

1 teaspoon baking powder

100 g/4 oz margarine or butter, diced

175 g/6 oz light soft brown sugar

175 g/6 oz dried apricots, chopped

150 ml/¼ pint milk

vegetable oil, for greasing

TOPPING

225 g/8 oz marzipan

icing sugar, for dusting

1 tablespoon apricot jam

25 g/1 oz split almonds

1 Heat the oven to 170C/325F/Gas 3. Grease a 10 × 20 cm/4 × 8 inch loaf tin and line with greased greaseproof paper.

2 Sift the flours and baking powder into a large bowl. Add the margarine or butter and rub in until the mixture resembles fine breadcrumbs. Stir in the sugar, apricots and milk and mix to a smooth batter.

3 Pour the mixture into the tin, smooth the surface and bake in the oven for 1½-1¾ hours until golden brown and a skewer inserted into the centre comes out clean. Leave in the tin for 5 minutes, then turn out on to a wire rack. Remove the lining paper and leave to cool completely.

4 Roll out the marzipan, on a work surface lightly dusted with icing sugar, to fit the top of the teabread. Brush the top of the teabread with jam and place the marzipan on top pressing gently to stick. Crimp the edges neatly then mark the marzipan with a diamond pattern using a sharp knife. Press the almonds into the marzipan and brown under a medium-hot grill. Leave to cool.

◆ Use pre-soaked apricots or soak very dry apricots in tepid water for a few hours and drain thoroughly before chopping.

Variation

◆ To make Banana and walnut teabread, add 50 g/ 2 oz chopped walnuts and 100 g/4 oz mashed banana to the mixture in place of the apricots and reduce the milk to 125 ml/4 fl oz. Omit the marzipan and almond topping.

Apple and ginger cake

Makes 24 slices

225 g/8 oz margarine or butter, softened

225 g/8 oz caster sugar

4 eggs, beaten

225 g/8 oz self-raising flour

2 teaspoons ground ginger

4 tablespoons milk

1 cooking apple about 225 g/8 oz, peeled, cored and chopped

vegetable oil, for greasing

1 Heat the oven to 190C/375F/Gas 5. Line the base and sides of a 20 × 30 cm/8 × 12 inch cake tin with greased greaseproof paper.

2 Place the margarine or butter and sugar in a bowl and beat until light and fluffy. Gradually beat in the eggs, beating well after each addition. Sift together the flour and ginger, fold into the creamed mixture with the milk, then stir in the apple. Spoon the mixture into the tin and smooth the surface.

3 Bake in the oven for 30-35 minutes or until golden brown and the top springs back when gently pressed. Let the cake cool in the tin for a few minutes, then turn out and peel off the lining paper. Leave on a wire rack to cool completely.

◆ The cake can be frozen for up to 3 months. Pack the slices in a rigid container, separating the layers with freezer tissue. Defrost at room temperature for 3-4 hours, then unwrap.

Variation

◆ For a crunchy topping, sprinkle 2 tablespoons of demerara sugar over the surface of the sponge mixture before baking.

Chocolate shortbread

Makes 8 slices

150 g/5 oz plain flour

pinch of salt

25 g/1 oz cocoa powder

50 g/2 oz caster sugar

100 g/4 oz margarine or butter, diced

caster sugar, for sprinkling

1 Heat the oven to 180C/350F/Gas 4.
2 Sift the flour, salt and cocoa into a bowl and add the margarine or butter and sugar. Work the ingredients together using one hand until the mixture forms a soft dough.
3 Roll out on a floured surface to a 20 cm/8 inch round and crimp the edge neatly. Prick the shortbread all over with a fork, then mark into 8 wedges. Transfer to a baking sheet.
4 Bake in the oven for 45 minutes. Remove the shortbread from the oven, sprinkle the top with caster sugar and cut into wedges with a sharp knife. Leave to cool for a few minutes, then transfer to a wire rack to cool completely.

◆ The shortbread dough can be made in a food processor. Place all the ingredients in the bowl and process until the mixture comes together into a smooth ball.

Variation
◆ For shortbread fingers; roll out the dough to 1 cm/½ inch, cut into 2.5 × 7.5 cm/1 × 3 inch fingers and prick with a fork. Bake for 20 minutes.

Honey nut flapjacks

Makes 8

75 g/3 oz margarine or butter, diced

100 g/4 oz demerara sugar

50 g/2 oz honey

150 g/5 oz rolled oats

25 g/1 oz chopped mixed nuts

vegetable oil, for greasing

1 Heat the oven to 180C/350F/Gas 4. Grease an 18 cm/7 inch sandwich tin and line the base with greased greaseproof paper.
2 Place the margarine or butter, sugar and honey in a saucepan. Heat gently, stirring occasionally until the sugar dissolves. Add the rolled oats and nuts and stir until well mixed. Spoon the mixture into the tin and smooth the surface.
3 Bake in the oven for about 20 minutes or until golden brown. Cool for 5 minutes, then cut into 8 wedges with a sharp knife.
4 Leave flapjacks to cool completely, then remove from the tin.

◆ Store the flapjacks in an airtight tin for up to 3 weeks.

◆ The flapjack mixture is very soft when first removed from the oven so be sure to cut right through to the base before it cools or the wedges will stick together.

Variation
◆ Use 175 g/6 oz muesli in place of the rolled oats and nuts.

Carrot cake

Makes 12 slices

225 g/8 oz grated carrot

125 ml/4 fl oz vegetable oil

100 g/4 oz light soft brown sugar

2 tablespoons clear honey

2 eggs

100 g/4 oz plain flour

100 g/4 oz wholewheat flour

1 teaspoon bicarbonate of soda

pinch of salt

2 teaspoons ground cinnamon

vegetable oil, for greasing

1 Heat the oven to 180C/350F/Gas 4. Grease a deep 20 cm/8 inch cake tin and line the base with greased greaseproof paper.

2 Place the carrot, oil, sugar, honey and eggs in a bowl and mix well. Sift together the flours, bicarbonate of soda, salt and cinnamon. Add to the carrot mixture and stir until well blended.

3 Spoon the mixture into the tin and smooth the surface. Bake in the oven for 40-50 minutes until golden brown and a skewer inserted into the centre comes out clean. Leave in the tin for a few minutes then turn out on to a wire rack to cool.

Variations

◆ Add 75 g/3 oz chopped nuts, sultanas or chopped dates to the carrot mixture with the flour.

◆ If eating the cake at home, it is delicious topped with cream cheese icing; beat together 40 g/1½ oz each of butter and cream cheese, then beat in 75 g/3 oz sifted icing sugar and a few drops of vanilla essence. Spread over the top of the cake. Decorate with a ring of finely pared carrot strips, if wished.

Raspberry yoghurt pots

Makes 4

300 ml/½ pint milk

1 tablespoon agar-agar powder

225 g/8 oz soft white cheese

150 ml/¼ pint natural yoghurt

100 g/4 oz caster sugar

2 tablespoons lime juice

1 egg, separated

225 g/8 oz raspberries

3 tablespoons redcurrant jelly

1 Heat the milk in a saucepan until boiling. Sprinkle the agar-agar over the milk, whisking continuously. Whisk until dissolved.

2 Mix together the cheese, yoghurt, sugar and lime juice. Stir in the hot milk mixture, then beat in the egg yolk. Mash half the raspberries and fold into the mixture.

3 Whisk the egg white until standing in soft peaks, fold into the mixture, then spoon into 4 yoghurt pots or plastic tubs. Place in the refrigerator for 2 hours or until set.

4 Arrange the remaining raspberries over the yoghurt mixture. Place the redcurrant jelly in a small pan and heat gently to melt. Spoon over the raspberries to coat completely and leave to set.

5 Cover the pots with cling film and pack tightly together in a rigid container.

Variation

◆ Use other fresh fruits such as strawberries, blackberries, or canned fruits such as apricots or peaches.

Carrot cake

Fruit tartlets

Makes 12

175 g/6 oz plain flour

pinch of salt

75 g/3 oz margarine or butter

about 3 tablespoons water

FILLING

1 egg, separated

25 g/1 oz caster sugar

150 ml/¼ pint milk

15 g/½ oz cornflour

few drops of vanilla essence

36 grapes, halved and seeded, or fruit of choice

4 tablespoons redcurrant jelly

1 tablespoon lemon juice

1 Heat the oven to 190C/375F/Gas 5.

2 Sift the flour and salt into a bowl. Add the margarine or butter and rub in until the mixture resembles fine breadcrumbs. Mix in just enough water to make a soft elastic dough. Wrap the dough in cling film and refrigerate for 30 minutes.

3 Roll out the pastry on a floured surface and cut out 12 rounds, using a 7.5 cm/3 inch fluted cutter; re-rolling the dough if necessary.

4 Use the pastry rounds to line 12 tart moulds. Prick the base and sides of each pastry case with a fork, then line each case with a piece of greaseproof paper and fill with baking beans.

5 Bake in the oven for 10 minutes, remove the paper and beans: bake 5-10 minutes more. Cool pastry cases on a wire rack.

6 Meanwhile, make the filling: place the egg yolk and sugar in a bowl and whisk until creamy. In a small bowl, mix 2 tablespoons of the milk with the cornflour and blend to a smooth paste. Heat the remaining milk until almost boiling, then stir into the cornflour mixture. Add the egg yolk mixture, stir thoroughly, then return to the pan.

7 Cook over a gentle heat until thickened, stirring continuously. Whisk the egg white until holding soft peaks and fold into the custard. Add the vanilla essence and leave to cool.

8 Divide custard between pastry cases. Level each surface and top with 6 grape halves.

9 Place the jelly and lemon juice in a small pan and heat gently until dissolved. Cool for about 5 minutes. Brush over the fruit and leave to set.

Cherry and almond baklava

Makes about 16 pieces

225 g/8 oz unsalted butter

400 g/14 oz packet frozen phyllo pastry, defrosted

175 g/6 oz blanched almonds, chopped

225 g/8 oz cherries, stoned and quartered

SYRUP

350 g/12 oz sugar

450 ml/¾ pint water

1 tablespoon lemon juice

2 tablespoons rose water

1 Heat the oven to 180C/350F/Gas 4.

2 Melt the butter and use a little to brush over the base of a 2.5 cm/1 inch deep 20 × 30 cm/8 × 12 inch baking tin.

3 Unroll the phyllo pastry sheets and cut in half crossways. Peel off a sheet of pastry and place in the tin, folding in the edges to fit if necessary. Brush the pastry with a little melted butter.

4 Repeat with one-third of the pastry sheets.

5 Mix the almonds and cherries together and sprinkle half the mixture over the pastry in the tin.

6 Continue layering and buttering another third of the pastry sheets, then sprinkle the remaining almonds and cherries over the top. Finish layering and buttering the remaining pastry, brushing the final layer with all of the remaining butter.

7 Using a large sharp knife, cut the pastry into about 16 diamond shapes. Bake in the oven for 30 minutes, then reduce the temperature to 150C/300F/Gas 2 and bake for a further 1 hour.

8 Make the syrup: place the sugar, water, lemon juice and rose water in a saucepan and heat gently, stirring occasionally, until the sugar has dissolved, then boil syrup for 10 minutes.

9 Cool slightly and spoon over the baklava until it has all been absorbed. Leave the baklava overnight before serving.

◆ Ready-made frozen phyllo pastry is available from delicatessens and shops specializing in Middle-eastern foods. There are about 20 sheets in a 400 g/14 oz packet. Defrost the sheets in the packet at room temperature for 3 hours. Keep covered to prevent drying out.

Variation

◆ Omit the cherries and use 275 g/10 oz chopped nuts instead. Pistachio nuts, brazil nuts or hazelnuts are all suitable.

Wholewheat bakewell tart

Makes 10 slices

3 tablespoons apricot jam

75 g/3 oz margarine or butter, softened

75 g/3 oz muscovado sugar

1 large egg, beaten

75 g/3 oz 81% wholewheat self-raising flour

½ teaspoon baking powder

75 g/3 oz ground almonds

PASTRY

175 g/6 oz wholewheat flour

pinch of salt

75 g/3 oz margarine or butter, diced

about 3 tablespoons water

1 Heat the oven to 190C/375F/Gas 5.

2 Make the pastry: sift the flour and salt into a bowl. Add the margarine or butter and rub in until the mixture resembles fine breadcrumbs. Mix in just enough water to make a soft elastic dough. Wrap the dough in cling film and refrigerate for 30 minutes.

3 Roll out the pastry on a floured surface and use to line a shallow 18 cm/7 inch square tin. Spread the base of the pastry case with apricot jam.

4 Place the margarine or butter and sugar in a bowl and beat until light and fluffy; beat in the egg. Sift together the flour and baking powder, then fold into the creamed mixture with the almonds.

5 Spoon the mixture into the pastry case and smooth the surface. Bake in the oven for 35-40 minutes until the top springs back when gently pressed. Leave to cool in the tin, then turn out and cut into 10 slices.

Variation

◆ For a nutty topping sprinkle the sponge with 25 g/1 oz flaked almonds before baking.

Orange and pineapple jellies

Makes 6

6 large oranges

425 g/15 oz can pineapple pieces in natural juice

about 150 ml/¼ pint fresh orange juice

4 tablespoons agar-agar flakes

1 Cut the tops from the oranges and reserve. Using a grapefruit knife and teaspoon, scoop out the flesh into a sieve over a 1 L/2 pint measuring jug. Squeeze the juice into the jug. Trim the bases of the orange skins, if necessary, to enable them to stand up and set aside.

2 Drain the pineapple, chop and reserve. Add the juice to the strained orange juice and make up to 750 ml/1¼ pints with the fresh orange juice.

3 Pour the juice into a saucepan and add the agar-agar flakes. Bring to the boil, stirring occasionally, then reduce the heat and simmer for 2 minutes. Stir to ensure the agar-agar flakes have completely dissolved.

4 Return the juice to the jug and add the pineapple pieces. Cool, stirring occasionally until the jelly begins to thicken. Divide the jelly between the orange skins and refrigerate until completely set, then replace the lids. Wrap the oranges individually in cling film and pack in a rigid container.

◆ Make sure that the jelly is quite thick before pouring it into the orange skins, so that the pineapple does not sink to the bottom.

SALADS

Raw vegetables are an important part of a vegetarian diet and they can be used in endless combinations to make summer salads. As well as traditional salad ingredients like lettuce, cucumber and tomato, try fennel, endive, radicchio and asparagus.

Shoots from alfalfa, mung (bean sprouts) and aduki beans add a lovely crunchy texture to salads, and are full of vitamins – alfalfa contains numerous vitamins.

Main meals and side salads

A salad can be a meal on its own or an accompaniment to a main course. Include some protein in the form of rice, wheat grains, pulses, pasta, nuts, cheese or eggs to make it a substantial and well balanced meal. Side salads can also be served as starters if wished.

Dressing a salad

The most basic combination of vegetables can be transformed by a good dressing. It's worth experimenting with different oils and vinegars. Olive oil with its distinctive strong flavour is the favourite oil for dressings. Sunflower and safflower are also good for dressings, particularly when there is fruit in the salad – their light, bland flavour does not overpower the fruit. These two oils also have the added advantage of being high in polyunsaturated fat and low in saturated fat (it is saturated fat that health experts advise we cut down on). Walnut oil is the most expensive oil, but it does have a deliciously nutty flavour which is particularly good in strong flavoured dressings such as a blue cheese dressing (see Radicchio and walnut salad with blue cheese dressing, page 70).

Wine, cider or herb vinegars are the best for salads; malt vinegar has a rather strong, harsh taste which can drown the flavour of vegetables.

Most leafy salads should only be dressed just before serving or they will be limp and soggy. Salads such as Three-bean salad (see page 75) can be dressed while still warm so the flavour of the dressing can be absorbed.

Garlic can be overpowering in a dressing; for a pleasantly mild taste cut a garlic clove in half and rub the cut side round the inside of the salad bowl before adding the salad.

Garnishes

Garnishes can be as simple or as elegant as you wish. The easiest garnish is a sprinkling of chopped fresh herbs or finely chopped nuts over the top of the salad.

For a more elegant effect, try radish roses or accordions, spring onion tassels, onion chrysanthemums or gherkin fans.

To make radish roses: cut a narrow slice from the root end of each radish, then cut thin petals from stem to root. For an accordion, make cuts almost through each radish. Soak the radishes in a bowl of iced water until they open out. For spring onion tassels, cut the onions into 5-7.5 cm/2-3 inch lengths, then make lengthways cuts halfway down each piece. Soak in chilled water to open out. Make onion chrysanthemums by cutting through button onions many times, then leaving in chilled water until the petals open out. Cut long thin gherkins lengthways into thin slices leaving the slices joined at one end. Make them into a fan by spreading out the slices until they overlap slightly.

Front: Chicory, alfalfa and peach salad.
Back: Radicchio and walnut salad.

Radicchio and walnut salad with blue cheese dressing

Serves 6
1 head radicchio
1 head endive
50 g/2 oz walnut halves
BLUE CHEESE DRESSING
1 egg yolk
½ teaspoon granulated sugar
½ teaspoon mustard powder
salt and freshly ground black pepper
1 tablespoon white wine vinegar
75 ml/3 fl oz walnut oil
50 ml/2 fl oz sunflower oil
75 ml/3 fl oz soured cream
50 g/2 oz Danish Blue cheese, crumbled

1 Make the dressing: put the egg yolk into a bowl with the sugar, mustard and salt and pepper to taste. Mix 1 teaspoon vinegar, then add the oils, drop by drop, whisking all the time, until the mayonnaise is thick and smooth. Gradually whisk in the remaining vinegar.

2 Set aside 50 ml/2 fl oz of the mayonnaise – this will not be needed and can be used for another salad.

3 Put the remaining mayonnaise into a bowl with the soured cream and blue cheese. Mix well together.

4 Tear the radicchio and endive into bite-sized pieces. Arrange in a salad bowl and scatter the walnuts over the top. Spoon over the dressing and serve at once.

Asparagus and avocado vinaigrette

Serves 6
500 g/1 lb asparagus
2 avocados
lemon twists, to garnish
VINAIGRETTE
5 tablespoons olive oil
1 tablespoon sesame oil
1 tablespoon lemon juice
1 tablespoon tarragon vinegar
½ teaspoon granulated sugar
½ teaspoon mustard powder
1 teaspoon chopped fresh tarragon
salt and freshly ground black pepper
TO GARNISH
lemon twists

1 Tie the asparagus in 2 bundles. Cover the tips with foil, then stand them upright in a saucepan of boiling salted water and cook for 10-15 minutes until tender.

2 Remove the asparagus from the pan and drain well. Remove the string and arrange the asparagus on a serving plate. Leave to cool.

3 Meanwhile, make the vinaigrette: put all the ingredients in a bowl or screw-topped jar and whisk or shake until well blended.

4 To serve: halve the avocados, peel and remove the stones. Cut the flesh into slices and arrange on the serving plate with the asparagus.

5 Pour over the vinaigrette, garnish with lemon twists and serve at once.

Chicory, alfalfa and peach salad

Serves 6

2 heads chicory

175 g/6 oz alfalfa sprouts

2 peaches

50 g/2 oz cashew nuts

DRESSING

1 tablespoon cider vinegar

3 tablespoons sunflower oil

1 teaspoon made English mustard

1 teaspoon caster sugar

salt and freshly ground black pepper

1 Make the dressing: put all the ingredients in a bowl or screw-topped jar and whisk or shake well together.

2 Cut off the chicory roots and rinse the leaves, discarding any damaged outer leaves.

3 Arrange the alfalfa in a round serving dish, then lay the chicory leaves like the spokes of a wheel on top.

4 Peel the peaches: put them in a bowl, pour over boiling water and leave for 30 seconds, then peel off the skins.

5 Cut the peaches in half, remove the stones, then cut the flesh into slices and arrange them on top of the chicory. Scatter the cashew nuts over the top.

6 Pour over the dressing and serve at once.

Green bean salad with tomato dressing

Serves 6

350 g/12 oz green beans, topped and tailed

DRESSING

225 g/8 oz tomatoes, roughly chopped

2 tablespoons tarragon vinegar

3 tablespoons sunflower oil

1 tablespoon chopped fresh tarragon

salt and freshly ground black pepper

TO GARNISH

2 spring onions, white parts only

flat-leaved parsley or coriander sprigs

1 Cook the beans in lightly salted water for about 5 minutes until tender but still crisp. Drain and leave to cool.

2 Make the dressing: purée the tomatoes in a blender or food processor, then press through a sieve to remove the seeds.

3 Put the purée into a saucepan and boil for 2-3 minutes to reduce slightly. Stir in the remaining ingredients, pour into a bowl and leave until cold.

4 Arrange the beans on a serving dish. Whisk the dressing and pour over the beans. Slice the spring onions into thin rings and scatter over the top. Garnish with flat-leaved parsley or coriander and serve at once.

◆ This salad makes a delicious summer starter served with hot crusty garlic or herb bread (see page 16). If you are not barbecuing, heat the bread in the oven at 200C/400F/Gas 6 for 10-15 minutes until heated through.

Fennel and apple salad

Serves 6

1 head fennel

1 garlic clove

1 head curly endive

3 celery stalks, chopped

2 dessert apples

1-2 teaspoons lemon juice

DRESSING

2 tablespoons olive oil

1 tablespoon sunflower oil

1 tablespoon cider vinegar

salt and freshly ground black pepper

1 Make the dressing: put all the ingredients in a bowl or screw-topped jar and whisk or shake until well blended.

2 Cut off the feathery leaves of the fennel and set aside for garnishing. Slice off the base, then chop the fennel.

3 Cut the garlic clove in half and rub the cut edges around the inside of the salad bowl.

4 Tear the endive into bite-sized pieces and arrange in the bowl. Scatter over the fennel and celery.

5 Core and chop the apples, then dip into the lemon juice. Add to the salad.

6 Pour over the dressing and garnish with the reserved fennel leaves.

Pasta salad

Serves 6

500 g/1 lb wholewheat pasta shapes (see below)

1 teaspoon olive oil

100 g/4 oz mange tout

½ green pepper, deseeded and cut into thin rings

½ red pepper, deseeded and cut into thin rings

100 g/4 oz button mushrooms, sliced

6 spring onions, sliced

2 eggs, hard-boiled and cut into wedges

DRESSING

2 tablespoons sunflower oil

1 tablespoon white wine vinegar

2 tablespoons chopped fresh mint

½ teaspoon caster sugar

salt and freshly ground black pepper

1 Make the dressing: put all the ingredients in a bowl or screw-topped jar and whisk or shake until well blended.

2 Bring a saucepan of salted water to the boil, add the olive oil and pasta and cook for 10-15 minutes, until the pasta is just tender. Drain and rinse under cold running water and drain again.

3 Meanwhile, cook the mange tout in boiling salted water for 2-3 minutes, drain and rinse under cold running water. Blanch the pepper rings in boiling water for 30 seconds. Rinse and drain.

4 Put the pasta in a large serving bowl and stir in the mange tout, pepper rings, mushrooms and spring onions. Arrange the hard-boiled egg wedges on the top. Pour over the dressing and serve.

◆ Any small pasta shapes can be used for this salad: wholewheat wheat ears or shells look particularly attractive.

Greek salad

Serves 6

1 cucumber, thinly sliced

225 g/8 oz tomatoes, thinly sliced

2 hard-boiled eggs, thinly sliced in rounds

100 g/4 oz pitted black olives

175 g/6 oz Feta cheese, cut into small cubes

6 thin slices green pepper

DRESSING

6 tablespoons olive oil

1 tablespoon lemon juice

1 tablespoon chopped fresh oregano or ½ teaspoon dried oregano

1 Arrange the cucumber slices in a ring around the edge of a round serving plate.

2 Place the tomato slices in a ring inside the cucumber slices, then arrange the egg slices inside the tomato ring, and the pepper slices in the centre. Sprinkle the olives and Feta cheese over the top of the salad.

3 Make the dressing: put all the ingredients in a bowl or a screw-topped jar and whisk or shake until well blended.

4 Pour the dressing over the salad and serve at once.

◆ Do not pour the dressing over the salad until ready to serve or the tomatoes and cucumber will become soggy.

Bulgar wheat salad

Serves 6

225 g/8 oz bulgar wheat

225 g/8 oz tomatoes, chopped

½ cucumber, diced

2 tablespoons chopped fresh mint

6 tablespoons chopped fresh parsley

2 garlic cloves, crushed

6 tablespoons olive oil

juice of 1 lemon

salt and freshly ground black pepper

lettuce leaves, to serve

1 Put the bulgar wheat in a bowl and cover with boiling water. Leave for 45 minutes, then place in a sieve and press down well to get rid of the excess water. Transfer the wheat to a bowl.

2 Stir in the tomatoes, cucumber and herbs. In a small bowl, mix together the garlic, oil, lemon juice and salt and pepper to taste.

3 Arrange the lettuce leaves on a serving dish and pile the bulgar wheat in the centre. Pour over the dressing and serve at once.

Orange rice ring

Serves 6

250 ml/8 fl oz orange juice

275 ml/9 fl oz water

225 g/8 oz brown rice, rinsed

75 g/3 oz Macadaemia or cashew nuts, chopped

4 spring onions, chopped

25 g/1 oz desiccated coconut

1 tablespoon thick mayonnaise

15 g/½ oz salad cress

salt and freshly ground black pepper

sunflower oil, for greasing

TO GARNISH

orange slices

watercress sprigs

1 Grease a 600 ml/½ pint plain or fluted ring mould.

2 Put the orange juice and water into a saucepan and bring to the boil. Add the rice, cover and simmer gently for 30 minutes until the rice is tender and the liquid has been absorbed. If the liquid is absorbed before the rice is tender, turn off the heat and leave the rice in the saucepan, covered, for 10-15 minutes.

3 Mix in the chopped nuts, spring onions, desiccated coconut, mayonnaise and cress. Season to taste with salt and pepper.

4 Spoon the mixture into the greased mould, pressing down well. Leave until cold, then chill in the refrigerator.

5 To serve: place a plate upside down over the mould, then invert the mould and plate, giving a shake halfway round. Garnish the centre and base of the ring with orange slices and watercress sprigs.

Three-bean salad

Serves 6

100 g/4 oz dried haricot beans, soaked overnight

100 g/4 oz dried kidney beans, soaked overnight

100 g/4 oz fresh broad beans (podded weight)

3 celery stalks, chopped

½ red pepper, deseeded and chopped

½ green pepper, deseeded and chopped

2 tablespoons finely chopped fresh herbs eg mint, chives and tarragon

DRESSING

½ onion, finely chopped

4 tablespoons chopped fresh parsley

1 garlic clove, crushed

1 teaspoon French mustard

1 tablespoon lemon juice

salt and freshly ground black pepper

50 ml/2 fl oz olive oil

1 Cook the haricot and kidney beans in separate saucepans of boiling water. Boil vigorously for 10 minutes, then simmer the haricot beans for about 1 hour and the kidney beans for about 40 minutes until tender. Do not add salt as this toughens the skins.

2 Meanwhile, cook the broad beans in lightly salted boiling water for about 15 minutes until tender.

3 Make the dressing: in a bowl, mix together the onion, parsley, garlic, mustard and lemon juice. Season well, then add the olive oil drop by drop, beating until thick.

4 Drain the beans, mix together in a large serving bowl and pour over the dressing while the beans are still hot.

5 Add the celery, peppers and herbs. Stir well until all the ingredients are coated in dressing. Leave until cold.

ENTERTAINING

The great advantage with summer entertaining is that some – if not all – the courses can be prepared ahead and served cold. It's worth planning your menu so that it includes at least one course that needs nothing more than a last minute garnish or swirl of cream.

Starting with a chilled soup is a certain success when the temperature is soaring. In the summer months there are so many tender young vegetables to choose from and they can be puréed in just a few seconds in a blender or food processor. Add a few fresh herbs from the garden, or spices, for extra flavour and then simply chill the soup until ready to serve.

Pâtés and dips are equally easy to make with fresh vegetables, pulses or cheese. They can either be served informally with a pre-meal drink or served as a starter for a more formal dinner. The selection in this chapter includes the classic Guacamole made with avocados, Fennel and carrot dip, Curried tomato and onion, Mushroom and aubergine pâté and Party vegetable terrine.

Outdoor eating
Summer entertaining hopefully means eating out of doors. Patio tables are perfect for entertaining small numbers in the garden, but if there are more than about four people it is likely that guests will eat standing up or perched on a garden chair. They are likely to be balancing a drink in one hand and food in the other, so it must be something that can be eaten easily with a fork or fingers. Large pepper rings and whole lettuce leaves may look very attractive on a serving plate but they are impossible to eat one-handed with a fork. If the food cannot be cut up with a fork, try to serve it bite-sized so that it doesn't have to be cut. Vegetable mousses such as Carrot and watercress mousse or Tomato and Cucumber jelly ring (see page 99) are ideal fork foods.

The fork foods section also includes some hot dishes for informal indoor entertaining when the weather is not so good, such as Summer vegetable gougère (see page 102), Tofu, mange tout and corn stir-fry (see page 96), Lentil and mushroom lasagne (see page 95) and two different kinds of crêpes – Wholewheat spinach and asparagus crêpes (see page 101) and Buckwheat courgette and corn crêpes (see page 102).

Canapés and finger foods
Canapés and finger foods – whether they are for indoor or outdoor eating – should be bite-sized for easy eating. Bases can be pastry – either shortcrust, puff, choux or phyllo – or bread, toast, small crisp crackers and biscuits. They can be topped with an endless variety of vegetable mixtures, cheese and nuts.

Summer desserts
A cool refreshing dessert is always welcome in summer. Lush seasonal fruits, so delicious served with a thick dollop of cream, can also be made into a tantalising array of desserts such as Three-berry mousse (see page 115), Tropical fruit mille feuille (see page 114) and Passionfruit Pavlova (see page 107). Also included in this chapter are delicious non-fruit desserts like Chocolate rum gateau and Brandy snaps with coffee cream (see page 108).

Tomato avocado lilies

PARTY CANAPES

These tempting bite-sized nibbles will disappear as fast as you arrange them on the serving plates. Vegetarians and non-vegetarians alike will love the tasty toppings on a variety of different bases. Most can be prepared ahead and need only a last minute garnish before serving.

Canapé platter

Makes 24 (4 per serving)

24 small, crisp crackers or biscuits (or use small rounds of toast)

a little butter, for spreading

PIQUANT CREAM CHEESE SPREAD

100 g/4 oz cream cheese

1 tablepoons tomato purée

2 pickled onions, finely chopped

4 stuffed olives, finely chopped

2 cocktail gherkins, finely chopped

EGG AND WATERCRESS SPREAD

2 hard-boiled eggs, shelled

½ bunch watercress, stalks trimmed, finely chopped

3 tablespoons mayonnaise

2 spring onions, trimmed and finely chopped

salt and freshly ground black pepper

1 Spread the crackers with butter.
2 Make the piquant cream cheese spread: put all the ingredients into a bowl and mix well together until thoroughly combined.
3 Make the egg and watercress spread: mash the hard-boiled eggs until smooth. Add the finely chopped watercress, mayonnaise and spring onions and season to taste with salt and pepper mix well.

4 Spread the cream cheese mixture on to 12 buttered crackers and the egg and watercress mixture on to the remaining 12 crackers.
5 Arrange crackers on a flat serving platter.

◆ Garnish the crackers attractively with a selection of the following: tiny radish roses and fresh herbs; black or green grapes; thin slices of radish and slices of button mushroom; thin slices of tomato and cucumber; dainty slices of avocado, brushed with lemon juice; gherkin fans and a dainty twist of lemon or lime.

Variations

◆ Cheesy mushroom spread: melt 15 g/½ oz butter in a saucepan. Add 50 g/2 oz sliced button mushrooms and 1 small peeled and chopped onion. Cook gently for 5 minutes. While still warm, put into a blender or food processor with 80 g/2.8 oz packet smoked processed cheese with mushroom. Process until finely blended. Season to taste with salt and freshly ground black pepper. Cool before using.

◆ Butter bean spread: purée together in a blender or food processor the following: ½ × 227 g/8 oz can butter beans (drained), 2 teaspoons olive oil, 2 teaspoons tomato purée, 1 garlic clove, 2 teaspoons lemon juice, 1 shallot, 1 carrot and salt and freshly ground black pepper to taste.

Stuffed egg mayonnaise whirls

Makes 12

6 eggs

4 tablespoons mayonnaise

½ teaspoon made English mustard

salt and freshly ground black pepper

6 gherkin slices

6 radish slices

1 Place the eggs in a small saucepan and cover with cold water. Bring to the boil, then simmer gently for 10 minutes. Drain, cool under cold running water and remove the shells.. Dry the eggs with absorbent paper.

2 Cut the hard-boiled eggs in half, remove the yolks and put into a bowl. Keep whites on one side. Mix the yolks with the mayonnaise, mustard and seasoning until smooth and well combined.

3 Place the mixture in a piping bag fitted with a large star nozzle and pipe the mixture into the hollows of the egg whites. Top 6 with gherkin slices and the remaining 6 with radish slices. Serve chilled.

Variations

◆ Replace the mustard with curry powder or tomato purée, if preferred.

◆ The eggs can be garnished with a sprinkling of chopped fresh parsley instead of the gherkin and radish slices, if preferred.

Party pizza

Serves 8

3 tablespoons olive oil

2 garlic cloves, crushed

2 large onions, chopped

400 g/14 oz can tomatoes

2 tablespoons tomato purée

1 teaspoon dried marjoram or oregano

salt and freshly ground black pepper

PASTRY

175 g/6 oz self-raising flour

100 g/4 oz wholewheat flour

½ teaspoon salt

150 g/5 oz margarine, cubed

4 tablespoons cold water

TOPPING

225 g/8 oz Mozzarella cheese, chopped

75 g/3 oz button mushrooms, sliced

1 green pepper, deseeded and cut into thin strips

15 black olives

1 tablespoon olive oil

1 teaspoon dried marjoram or oregano

1 Heat the olive oil in a saucepan. Add garlic and onions: fry gently for 3 minutes. Stir in tomatoes, tomato purée, marjoram and seasoning. Cook, uncovered, for 15 minutes, stirring occasionally.

2 Make the pastry: put the flours and salt into a bowl. Rub in the margarine until the mixture resembles breadcrumbs. Add the water and mix to form a firm dough. Chill for 15 minutes.

3 Heat oven to 190C/375F/Gas 5. Roll out pastry to a rectangle measuring 35 × 25 cm/14 × 10 inches. Using rolling pin, place in a 32 × 23 cm/13 × 9 inch Swiss roll tin. Press into corners, up the sides and over edges of tin. Trim with a sharp knife, then pinch the edges to give a neat border. Prick the base several times with a fork.

4 Spoon the cooked tomato mixture on to pastry. Scatter over Mozzarella. Arrange sliced mushrooms over half the pizza and pepper strips over other half. Decorate the surface with olives, then drizzle olive oil over. Sprinkle with marjoram and freshly ground black pepper.

5 Bake for 35-40 minutes until golden. Serve warm.

Party-time pinwheels

Makes 18

1 large unsliced brown or white sandwich loaf

25 g/1 oz butter, softened

WATERCRESS CHEESE FILLING

50 g/2 oz cream cheese

⅓ bunch watercress, trimmed and very finely chopped

1 teaspoon milk

AVOCADO FILLING

½ ripe avocado

¼ teaspoon malt vinegar

salt and freshly ground black pepper

CARROT FILLING

1 carrot

1 shallot

1 tablespoon mayonnaise

salt and freshly ground black pepper

1 Cut the crusts off the loaf, then cut off 3 lengthways slices, just under 1 cm/½ inch thick. (Freeze the remaining section of loaf to use as required.) Spread each slice with butter.

2 Make the watercress cheese filling: mix the cream cheese, watercress and milk together until soft and well combined.

3 Make the avocado filling: mash the avocado flesh and mix with vinegar and seasoning.

4 Make the carrot filling: very finely chop the carrot and shallot in a blender or food processor. Add the mayonnaise and seasoning and mix well.

5 Cover each slice of buttered bread with one of the fillings. Roll up each slice, like a Swiss roll (starting from a short side), then wrap each one tightly in cling film and chill for several hours, or overnight.

6 Cut each roll into 6 pinwheels and arrange in rows on a serving platter.

Back left: Piquant cream cheese canapés from the Canapé platter. Back right: Stuffed egg mayonnaise whirls. Front: Party-time pinwheels.

Phyllo spinach bites

Makes 12

175 g/6 oz frozen chopped spinach

75 g/3 oz butter

1 small onion, finely chopped

40 g/1½ oz wholemeal breadcrumbs

1 egg, beaten

finely grated zest of 1 small lemon

salt and freshly ground black pepper

6 sheets frozen phyllo pastry, defrosted

1 Heat the oven to 190C/375F/Gas 5.

2 Cook the spinach following the packet directions. Drain thoroughly, pressing out all the excess moisture.

3 Melt 25 g/1 oz butter in a saucepan, add the onion and cook gently for 5 minutes. Remove from heat. Stir in the spinach, breadcrumbs, beaten egg, lemon zest and seasoning. Mix well, then divide into 12 portions.

4 Melt the remaining butter in a pan, then remove from the heat. Work with one sheet of phyllo pastry at a time, keeping the remainder covered with a damp cloth. Cut the phyllo pastry sheet in half lengthways, then fold each portion in half lengthways.

5 Put a portion of spinach mixture in one corner of each piece of pastry and pat out lightly. Now fold pastry at right angles to make a triangle and brush with a little melted butter. Continue folding in this way along the pastry strip, brushing with melted butter between each fold, to form a neat triangular parcel. Brush with melted butter again and arrange on a greased baking sheet.

6 Repeat this procedure with the remaining sheets of pastry, spinach filling and melted butter, to make 12 parcels in all.

7 Bake for 20 minutes until golden brown and cooked through. Cover with foil during cooking, if necessary, to prevent pastry overbrowning. These should be served hot.

Tangy choux puffs

Makes 12

CHOUX PASTRY

32 g/1¼ oz plain flour

pinch of salt

65 ml/2½ fl oz water

22 g/¾ oz butter

1 egg, beaten

1 teaspoon poppy seeds

FILLING

1 dessert apple

100 g/4 oz curd cheese

1 tablespoon chopped fresh chives

¼-½ teaspoon curry powder, to taste

salt and freshly ground black pepper

2 teaspoons lemon juice

1 celery stalk, trimmed and finely chopped

1 Heat the oven to 200C/400F/Gas 6.

2 Make the pastry: sift the flour and salt on to a piece of greaseproof paper. Put the water and butter in a saucepan and heat gently until the butter has melted. (Do not allow water to boil before the butter has melted.) Bring to the boil, remove from heat and immediately add the flour, all at once, and stir quickly with a wooden spoon until smooth.

3 Return the pan to a moderate heat for a few moments and beat well until the dough forms a ball and leaves the sides of the pan clean. Remove from the heat and cool slightly. Gradually add the beaten egg, beating well after each addition until the mixture forms a shiny dough.

4 Place teaspoonfuls of the mixture on a lightly greased baking sheet, spacing them well apart. Sprinkle each one with poppy seeds.

5 Bake for 20-25 minutes until well risen and crisp. Make a small slit in the side of each one to allow steam to escape. Cool on a wire rack.

6 Make the filling: peel, core and grate the apple. Mix thoroughly with remaining filling ingredients. Cut choux puffs in half. Fill bases with the mixture and replace tops. Serve within 30 minutes of filling.

Variation

◆ Sprinkle choux puffs with sesame seeds or chopped nuts instead of poppy seeds, if wished.

Tomato avocado lilies

Serves 6

3 large firm tomatoes

1 large ripe avocado

100 g/4 oz cream cheese

few drops of Worcestershire sauce (see below)

½ teaspoon lemon juice

salt and freshly ground black pepper

parsley sprigs, to garnish

1 Insert a small, sharp pointed knife halfway between the stalk end and top of each tomato. Cut all the way round the tomato with a zig-zag motion, making sure you cut through the centre of tomato each time. Separate tomato into halves.

2 Carefully scoop out the seeds and juice from the tomatoes, taking care not to damage the shells. Leave the tomato shells to drain, upside down, on absorbent paper while preparing the filling.

3 Halve the avocado, remove the stone and scoop out the flesh. Mash the flesh well with a fork and mix with the cream cheese, Worcestershire sauce, lemon juice and seasoning.

4 Spoon the mixture into the tomato shells and garnish each one with a tiny parsley sprig.

◆ Look for a Worcestershire sauce that is anchovy-free.

Variation
◆ Replace the cream cheese with curd cheese or sieved cottage cheese, if preferred.

Cheesy sesame bites

Makes 24

400 g/14 oz packet frozen puff pastry, defrosted

2 tablespoons hamburger relish

75 g/3 oz Cheddar cheese, grated

a little beaten egg or milk, to glaze

1 tablespoon sesame seeds

2 teaspoons grated Parmesan cheese

1 Heat the oven to 200C/400F/Gas 6. Roll out the pastry on a lightly floured surface to a 35 × 30 cm/14 × 12 inch rectangle and mark in half crossways.

2 Spread relish over one half to within 5 mm/¼ inch of the edges. Sprinkle over the grated cheese, then dampen the pastry edges with water. Fold the uncovered half over the cheesy half and press the edges together well to seal.

3 Brush with beaten egg or milk to glaze, then sprinkle with sesame seeds and Parmesan cheese. Press the pastry lightly and cut into 1 cm/½ inch wide strips. Loop each strip to form a knot and place on a dampened baking sheet.

4 Bake for 20-25 minutes until lightly golden. Serve hot or cold.

Variation
◆ Replace the sesame seeds with poppy seeds, if preferred.

SOUPS

Use a homemade vegetable stock for a well-flavoured soup.
Make the stock from any vegetables – carrots, potatoes, onions
and celery are particularly good. Add herbs and water and
simmer for about 2 hours, then strain off the stock. An
attractive garnish takes only minutes, but makes all the
difference to soup.

Corn and mushroom soup

Serves 6

2 tablespoons sunflower oil

1 bunch spring onions, trimmed and thinly sliced

100 g/4 oz button mushrooms, thinly sliced

1 garlic clove, crushed

1.1 L/2 pints vegetable stock

3 tablespoons light soy sauce

2 tablespoons dry sherry

411 g/14½ oz can creamed style corn

salt and freshly ground black pepper

1 Heat the oil in a saucepan, add the onions, mushrooms and garlic and fry gently for 2 minutes. Add the stock, soy sauce, sherry and creamed corn.
2 Bring to the boil, then cover and simmer for 5 minutes. Taste and adjust seasoning if necessary. Serve hot.

Tomato and basil soup

Serves 6

40 g/1½ oz butter or margarine

2 leeks, trimmed and shredded finely

1 potato, chopped

500 g/1 lb tomatoes, chopped

salt and freshly ground black pepper

1 tablespoon muscovado sugar

3 tablespoons tomato purée

1-2 tablespoons chopped fresh basil

750 ml/1¼ pint vegetable stock

300 ml/½ pint milk

300 ml/½ pint single cream

TO GARNISH

a little soured cream

basil sprigs

1 Melt the butter or margarine in a saucepan, add the leeks, potato, tomatoes and salt and pepper to taste and cook gently for 5 minutes, stirring occasionally.
2 Add the sugar, tomato purée, basil and stock and bring to the boil. Cover and simmer gently for 25-30 minutes until the vegetables are tender.
3 Purée the mixture in a blender or food processor. Sieve if necessary to remove any tomato seeds or skin. Leave to cool.
4 Stir in milk and cream. Adjust seasoning. Serve chilled with a spoonful of soured cream and sprigs of basil.

Tomato and basil soup

Iced Indian cucumber soup

Serves 6

25 g/1 oz butter or margarine

1 large onion, finely chopped

1 tablespoon garam masala

1½ cucumbers, grated (but not peeled)

25 g/1 oz plain flour

600 ml/1 pint vegetable stock

2 egg yolks

300 ml/½ pint single cream

salt and freshly ground black pepper

150 ml/¼ pint natural yoghurt

150 ml/¼ pint milk

grated unpeeled cucumber, to garnish

1 Melt the butter or margarine in a saucepan, add the onion, garam masala and grated cucumber and fry gently for 5 minutes, stirring frequently. Stir in the flour and cook for 1 minute, then add the stock and bring to the boil, stirring. Cover and simmer gently for 10 minutes.

2 Beat the egg yolks with 150 ml/¼ pint single cream. Remove the soup from the heat and whisk in the cream and egg mixture. Add seasoning to taste, then pour into a bowl and leave to cool.

3 Stir in the yoghurt, remaining cream and the milk. Serve chilled, garnished with grated unpeeled cucumber.

Variations

◆ Reduce the quantity of cream to 150 ml/¼ pint and increase the milk to 300 ml/½ pint for a less rich soup.

◆ Add 1 teaspoon curry powder to the garam masala, if wished, for a stronger flavour.

Watercress soup

Serves 6

50 g/2 oz butter or margarine

2 bunches watercress, washed and stalks trimmed

1 large potato, chopped

1 large onion, chopped

1 tablespoon plain flour

900 ml/1½ pints vegetable stock

150 ml/¼ pint milk

150 ml/¼ pint single cream

salt and freshly ground black pepper

watercress leaves, to garnish

1 Melt the butter or margarine in a saucepan, add the watercress, potato and onion and cook gently for 5 minutes. Stir in the flour and cook for 1 minute, then add the stock and bring to the boil, stirring.

2 Cover and simmer gently for 25-30 minutes until the vegetables are tender. Allow to cool slightly, then purée in a blender or food processor until smooth. Leave to cool.

3 Stir in the milk and cream and season to taste with salt and pepper.

4 Serve chilled, garnished with watercress leaves.

Bortsch

Serves 6

50 g/2 oz butter or margarine

500 g/1 lb raw beetroot, peeled and grated

2 celery stalks, trimmed and finely chopped

1 onion, quartered and thinly sliced

2 carrots, grated

1 potato, diced

1.1 L/2 pints vegetable stock

1 bay leaf

150 ml/¼ pint soured cream

salt and freshly ground black pepper

TO GARNISH

chopped fresh parsley

swirls of soured cream

1 Melt the butter or margarine in a saucepan. Reserve a quarter of the grated beetroot for later. Add the remaining beetroot and other vegetables to the pan and cook gently for 5 minutes, stirring frequently.

2 Stir in the stock and bay leaf and bring to the boil, then cover and simmer for 30 minutes until all the vegetables are tender.

3 Add the reserved beetroot to pan and cook for 10 minutes. Remove from heat, discard bay leaf and leave the soup to cool.

4 Stir the soured cream into the cold soup, then taste and adjust seasoning, if necessary. Chill in the refrigerator. Serve chilled, garnished with chopped parsley and swirls of soured cream.

◆ The mixture may be puréed in a blender or food processor at the end of stage 3, if a smooth soup is preferred.

Gazpacho

Serves 6

1 large green pepper, deseeded and diced

1 Spanish onion, chopped

2 garlic cloves, chopped

½ cucumber, peeled and chopped

50 g/2 oz wholemeal breadcrumbs

2 tablespoons wine or malt vinegar

1 tablespoon tomato purée

2 × 400 g/14 oz cans tomatoes

6 tablespoons olive oil

2 tablespoons lemon juice

1 teaspoon muscovado sugar

salt and freshly ground black pepper

150 ml/¼ pint tomato juice

150 ml/¼ pint water

TO SERVE

small bowls of diced, unpeeled cucumber; diced, skinned tomatoes; wholewheat croûtons; chopped onions; pitted black olives

1 Put all the ingredients (except those for serving) into a bowl and mix well. Purée the mixture (one-third quantity at a time) in a blender or food processor until smooth.

2 Pour into a bowl and chill well. Serve the soup with small bowls of cucumber, tomatoes, croûtons, onions and olives.

DIPS AND PATES

Vegetarian pâtés seldom take more than a few minutes to make and don't usually need weighting down like meat ones. The dips included here are so quick they are almost instant. The addition of herbs, spices and seasoning is important in both vegetable pâtés and dips to ensure a well-flavoured dish.

Potted Dolcelatte

Serves 6

175 g/6 oz Dolcelatte

75 g/3 oz butter, softened

2 tablespoons port

3 tablespoons chopped fresh chives

40-50 g/1½-2 oz walnuts, coarsely chopped

halved black grapes to garnish

1 Beat the Dolcelatte, butter and port together until soft and creamy. Stir in the chopped chives and walnuts and mix together lightly but ensure it is thoroughly blended.
2 Turn the mixture into a serving bowl, cover and chill before serving. Garnish with the grape halves.

Curried tomato and onion dip

Serves 6

2 tablespoons corn oil

2 onions, chopped

1 garlic clove, chopped

1 teaspoon curry powder

½ teaspoon ground cumin

½ teaspoon ground coriander

400 g/14 oz can tomatoes

salt

25 g/1 oz creamed coconut

3 tablespoons soured cream

strips of fresh green chilli, to garnish

1 Heat the oil in a saucepan, add the onions, garlic and spices and cook gently for 5 minutes, stirring occasionally.
2 Stir in the tomatoes and break up with a spoon. Add salt to taste and bring the mixture to the boil, then simmer, uncovered, for 25 minutes.
3 Stir the creamed coconut into mixture, then remove from heat and leave to cool slightly. Purée the mixture in a blender or food processor until smooth, then leave to cool.
4 Stir in the soured cream, cover and chill before serving. Garnish with strips of fresh green chilli.

Potted Dolcelatte

Hummus

Serves 6

175 g/6 oz dried chick peas, soaked

5 tablespoons lemon juice

4 tablespoons olive oil

3 garlic cloves

3 tablespoons tahini (sesame cream)

6 tablespoons water

salt and freshly ground black pepper

TO SERVE

2 tablespoons olive oil

paprika, for sprinkling

pitted black olives

1 Drain the chick peas and rinse well then place in a saucepan, cover with cold water and bring to the boil. Reduce the heat and simmer for 2-2½ hours until tender. Drain well.

2 Mix together the chick peas, lemon juice, olive oil, garlic, tahini, water and plenty of seasoning to taste. Purée the mixture (a half quantity at a time) in a blender or food processor until smooth. Thin the consistency even further, if wished, with extra lemon juice.

3 Turn mixture into a serving dish, cover and chill before serving. Just before serving, spoon the 2 tablespoons olive oil over the hummus and sprinkle liberally with paprika. Garnish with a few pitted black olives.

Spicy lentil dip

Serves 6

25 g/1 oz butter or margarine

1 onion, finely chopped

175 g/6 oz split red lentils

300 ml/½ pint vegetable stock

150 ml/¼ pint orange juice, plus 2 tablespoons

½ teaspoon ground cinnamon

½ teaspoon paprika

1½ teaspoons chilli sauce

3 tablespoons single cream

TO GARNISH

coriander leaves

thin slices of orange

1 Melt the butter or margarine in a saucepan, add the onion and fry gently for 3 minutes. Add the lentils, stock, 150 ml/¼ pint orange juice, cinnamon, paprika and chilli sauce and bring to the boil. Stir well, then cover and simmer gently for 20 minutes until all the liquid has been absorbed.

2 Remove the pan from the heat and beat the mixture well with a wooden spoon. Stir in the remaining orange juice, then leave to cool.

3 Stir in the cream and taste and adjust the seasoning, if necessary. Cover and chill before serving. Garnish with fresh coriander leaves and thin slices of orange.

Guacamole

Serves 6

2 large avocados

1 tablespoon lemon juice

1 garlic clove, crushed

2 shallots, grated

1 tablespoon olive oil

¼ teaspoon Tabasco sauce

salt and freshly ground black pepper

cayenne pepper (optional)

1 Halve the avocados, remove the stones and scoop out the flesh. Mash flesh thoroughly until smooth and put into a bowl.
2 Add the lemon juice, crushed garlic, grated shallots, oil, Tabasco and salt and pepper to taste; add a pinch or two of cayenne pepper, if using. Mix all ingredients well together.
3 Turn into a serving dish, cover and chill until required.

Herbed cucumber cheese dip

Serves 6-8

1 large cucumber, peeled

500 g/1 lb cottage cheese

2 tablespoons chopped fresh herbs (a mixture of chives and parsley)

150 ml/¼ pint mayonnaise

1 teaspoon sugar

salt and freshly ground black pepper

150 ml/¼ pint soured cream

warm fingers of pitta bread, to serve

1 Cut the cucumber in half lengthways and remove the seeds. Cut up the cucumber and put into a blender or food processor; add the cottage cheese and herbs and process finely.
2 Turn the mixture into a bowl, add the mayonnaise, sugar, seasoning and soured cream and mix well together. Turn into a serving bowl and chill for several hours before serving with warm fingers of pitta bread.

Mushroom and aubergine pâté

Serves 6

350 g/12 oz aubergine

50 g/2 oz butter

1 onion, chopped

2 garlic cloves, chopped

175 g/6 oz flat mushrooms, peeled and cut up

salt and freshly ground black pepper

a good pinch cayenne pepper

3 tablespoons medium oatmeal

40 g/1½ oz unsalted cashew nuts

4 tablespoons chopped fresh chives

1 Prick the aubergine several times with a fork and cook at 190C/375F/Gas 5 for 30 minutes or until the aubergine feels tender when pierced with the point of a knife.
2 Meanwhile, melt 25 g/1 oz butter in a saucepan. Add the onion, garlic and mushrooms, and fry gently for 3 minutes. Season to taste with salt, pepper and cayenne, then cover and cook gently for 10 minutes. Stir in the oatmeal, cover and cook for a further 10 minutes, stirring frequently.
3 Cut the stalk end off the aubergine and cut the aubergine in half. Scoop out the flesh and put into a blender or food processor. Add the mushroom mixture and cashews and process until the mixture is smooth. Stir in 3 tablespoons chives, then taste and adjust the seasoning, if necessary.
4 Turn the mixture into a serving dish and level the surface. Melt the remaining butter in a pan, then remove from the heat and add the remaining chives. Pour the mixture over the surface of pâté and leave to cool. Chill for several hours before serving.

Party vegetable terrine

Serves 6-8

1 tablespoon corn oil, plus a little for brushing

1 onion, chopped

1 garlic clove, chopped

½ teaspoon dried marjoram

400 g/14 oz can tomatoes in tomato juice

salt and freshly ground black pepper

1 red pepper, cut in half and deseeded

2 small courgettes, trimmed and quartered lengthways

10 large spinach leaves, stalks trimmed

3 teaspoons agar-agar powder

100 g/4 oz cream cheese

½ × 350 g/12 oz can green asparagus spears, drained

DRESSING

6 tablespoons corn oil

2 tablespoons red wine or malt vinegar

1 garlic clove, crushed

¼ teaspoon made English mustard

½ teaspoon caster sugar or honey

salt and freshly ground black pepper

TO GARNISH

sprigs of fresh mint

radish quarters

1 Heat the 1 tablespoon oil in a saucepan, add the onion, garlic, marjoram, tomatoes and seasoning. Cover and simmer for 15 minutes.

2 Brush the pepper with the remaining oil and put on a baking sheet. Cook at 190C/375F/Gas 5 for 15 minutes until the skin wrinkles. Remove the skin from the pepper and cut the pepper into 1 cm/½ inch wide strips.

3 Cook the courgettes in boiling, salted water for 5 minutes, then refresh in cold water and drain well. Pat dry on absorbent paper.

4 Cook the spinach leaves in boiling, salted water for 2 minutes, then drain well. Refresh in cold water and drain well again. Pat dry on absorbent paper.

5 Add the agar-agar to the hot tomato mixture and boil for 1 minute, stirring frequently. Cool slightly, then purée the mixture in a blender or food processor until smooth. Add the cream cheese and blend again until well combined. Turn the mixture into a bowl and leave to cool for about 15 minutes, stirring occasionally.

6 Line a 500 g/1 lb, 900 ml/1½ pint capacity, loaf tin with cling film, allowing the cling film to overhang the rim of the tin. Arrange overlapping spinach leaves, veined-sides upwards, in the tin to cover the base and sides of tin and allowing the leaves to overlap the rim of tin each time.

7 Put 3 tablespoons of the tomato mixture in the lined tin and level the surface. Arrange the courgettes on top, cutting them to fit, if necessary. Cover with another 3 tablespoons of the tomato mixture and level the surface; top with the strips of red pepper. Cover again with 3 tablespoons tomato mixture and top with the asparagus spears. Add the remaining tomato mixture and level the surface. Fold the overlapping spinach leaves over the mixture and cover with cling film.

8 Chill for several hours or overnight. To serve, cut into 2 cm/¾ inch thick slices and arrange on plates.

9 Make the dressing: place all the ingredients in a screw-topped jar and shake vigorously until well blended. Spoon a little dressing around each slice to flood the plate and garnish each slice with a sprig of mint and radish quarters.

Party vegetable terrine

Butter bean pepper pâté

Serves 6

2 garlic cloves

4 spring onions, trimmed and cut up

425 g/15 oz can butter beans, drained

2 tablespoons olive oil

1 tablespoon lemon juice

2 tablespoons chopped fresh parsley

salt and freshly ground black pepper

65 g/2½ oz fresh wholemeal breadcrumbs

1 red pepper

1 green pepper

1 yellow pepper

1 Put the garlic, spring onions, butter beans and oil into a blender or food processor and process until the mixture forms a creamy purée. Add the lemon juice, parsley, seasoning and bread-crumbs and process again until smooth.

2 Cut a slice off the stalk end of each pepper and remove the seeds. Fill the peppers with the butter bean pâté, pressing the mixture in firmly. Level the surfaces, then wrap in cling film and chill for at least 2 hours before serving.

3 Cut the peppers into chunky slices and arrange them on a serving plate, alternating the different colours.

◆ This recipe is even nicer made the day before required, as this allows time for the flavours to mellow.

◆ Add a little more lemon juice, if needed, during step 1, to help prevent the mixture from jamming the processor (don't make the mixture too moist).

Fennel and carrot dip

Serves 6

1 medium fennel bulb, trimmed and cut up

4 carrots, cut up

3 spring onions, trimmed and cut up

2 egg yolks

2 teaspoons lemon juice

1 tablespoon wholegrain mustard

2 tablespoons corn oil

2 tablespoons double cream

3 tablespoons mayonnaise

1 teaspoon clear honey

salt and freshly ground black pepper

1 Chop the fennel, carrots and spring onions very finely in a food processor or with a sharp knife. Turn out on to absorbent paper and pat dry, then place in a bowl.

2 In a small bowl, blend the egg yolks with the lemon juice and mustard, then gradually beat in the oil and cream until well blended. Add this mixture to the vegetables in bowl and mix lightly.

3 Stir in the mayonnaise, honey and season to taste with salt and pepper. Toss well together. Cover and chill before serving.

FORK FOOD

For a buffet party, when guests are helping themselves, it is important that dishes like savoury mousses are garnished so that guests can distinguish between the sweet and the savoury: you'll find plenty of attractive garnish ideas in this section together with fork foods for all occasions.

Lentil and mushroom lasagne

Serves 6

3 tablespoons corn oil

1 large onion, chopped

175 g/6 oz button mushrooms, sliced

2 garlic cloves, crushed

1 green pepper, deseeded and chopped

225 g/8 oz split red lentils

400 g/14 oz can tomatoes

½-1 teaspoon dried marjoram

450 ml/¾ pint vegetable stock

2 tablespoons tomato purée

salt and freshly ground black pepper

9 sheets wholewheat lasagne or lasagne verdi

SAUCE

40 g/1½ oz butter or margarine

40 g/1½ oz plain flour

450 ml/¾ pint milk

100 g/4 oz Mozzarella cheese, chopped

50 g/2 oz Cheddar cheese, grated

2 eggs, beaten

1 Heat the oil in a saucepan and fry the onion, mushrooms, garlic, green pepper and lentils over gentle heat for 5 minutes, stirring occasionally. Stir in the tomatoes, marjoram, stock and tomato purée. Bring to the boil, then cover and simmer gently for 25-30 minutes until tender and liquid is absorbed. Season to taste.

2 Meanwhile, heat the oven to 180C/350F/Gas 4. Cook the lasagne sheets in a large saucepan of boiling, salted water for 8-10 minutes until just tender. Drain and rinse with cold water, then drain again and pat dry on absorbent paper.

3 Make the sauce: melt the butter or margarine in a pan, add the flour and cook for 1 minute. Stir in the milk and bring to the boil, stirring, then reduce heat and simmer for 2 minutes, stirring all the time. Remove from heat and stir in half the Mozzarella and Cheddar cheeses, then add the beaten eggs and seasoning and beat well together.

4 Place one-third of the sheets of lasagne in a 28 × 20 cm/11 × 8 inch greased shallow ovenproof dish and cover with half the lentil mixture. Cover this with half the prepared sauce. Place another one-third quantity of lasagne over sauce and top with the remaining lentil mixture. Cover with the remaining lasagne and finish with a layer of sauce on the top. Sprinkle with the remaining Mozzarella and Cheddar cheeses.

5 Bake for 40-45 minutes until the topping is set and golden brown. Leave to cool for 10 minutes, then cut into 6 portions and serve hot with a salad of your choice.

Variation

◆ If preferred, use continental brown lentils instead of the split red variety. Soak brown lentils for 30 minutes in enough boiling water to cover, before using. Although continental brown lentils retain their shape after cooking, they can be blended to a pulpy texture, if preferred.

Vegetable couscous

Serves 6

350 g/12 oz couscous
750 ml/1¼ pints water
3 tablespoons olive oil
2 onions, chopped
4 carrots, thinly sliced
2 garlic cloves, crushed
227 g/8 oz can tomatoes in tomato juice
1 aubergine, trimmed, quartered and sliced
3 courgettes, trimmed and sliced
½ teaspoon ground ginger
½ teaspoon ground coriander
½ teaspoon ground cumin
½ teaspoon ground cinnamon
½ teaspoon chilli seasoning
2 tablespoons tomato purée
salt
50 g/2 oz raisins
600 ml/1 pint vegetable stock
439 g/15½ oz can chick peas, drained
50 g/2 oz unsalted cashew nuts
2 tablespoons chopped fresh parsley

1 Put the couscous in a bowl and add the water. Soak for 15 minutes until water is absorbed.
2 Heat the oil in a large saucepan, add the onions, carrots and garlic and fry gently for 5 minutes, stirring occasionally. Stir in the tomatoes and break up with a spoon, then add the aubergine, courgettes, spices, tomato purée and season to taste with salt. Stir well, then add the raisins and stock. Bring to the boil and stir well.
3 Line a large metal sieve with muslin or a clean kitchen cloth and place over the vegetable stew. Put couscous in the sieve. Cover pan with foil to enclose the steam. Simmer for 20 minutes.
4 Add the chick peas, cashews and parsley to the vegetable stew, stir well, then replace the sieve and fluff up the couscous with a fork. Re-cover and simmer for a further 20 minutes.
5 Arrange the couscous on a warm serving platter and fluff up with a fork. Spoon the vegetable stew mixture on top. Serve hot.

Tofu, mange tout and corn stir-fry

Serves 6

3 tablespoons sunflower oil
1 large onion, halved and sliced thinly
1 fresh green chilli, deseeded and chopped
12 baby corn cobs
1 green pepper, deseeded and cut into thin strips
275 g/10 oz mange tout, topped and tailed
2 garlic cloves, crushed
250 g/9 oz packet tofu, drained and cut into cubes
2 teaspoons cornflour
150 ml/¼ pint vegetable stock
2 tablespoons soy sauce
2 tablespoons sherry
salt and freshly ground black pepper
boiled rice or noodles, to serve

1 Heat the oil in a large frying pan or wok. Add the onion, chilli, corn cobs and green pepper and stir-fry over medium heat for 5 minutes. Add the mange tout, garlic and tofu and stir-fry for a further 5 minutes. Remove ingredients from pan with a draining spoon and turn into a warm serving dish; keep warm.
2 Blend the cornflour with a little of the stock, then add the remaining stock, soy sauce and sherry. Add to the pan and bring to the boil, stirring all the time. Reduce the heat and simmer for 2 minutes, stirring. Add seasoning to taste and pour over vegetable mixture in serving dish. Toss lightly together and serve hot with boiled rice or noodles.

Tofu, mange tout and corn stir-fry

Ratatouille pasta

Serves 6

1 large aubergine, trimmed, quartered and sliced
3 courgettes, trimmed and sliced
2 teaspoons salt
6 tablespoons olive oil
1 large onion, halved and sliced
2 garlic cloves, crushed
1 green pepper, deseeded and cut into thin strips
1 red pepper, deseeded and cut into thin strips
3 large tomatoes, skinned and chopped
freshly ground black pepper
225 g/8 oz green tagliatelle noodles
40 g/1½ oz butter
salt
25 g/1 oz fresh brown breadcrumbs
25 g/1 oz Cheddar or Parmesan cheese, grated
garlic bread, to serve

1 Put aubergine and courgettes in layers in a colander (standing on a plate) and sprinkle each layer with salt. Leave for 1 hour.

2 Rinse aubergine and courgettes under cold running water and pat dry on absorbent paper.

3 Heat the oil in a saucepan, add the onion, garlic, peppers, aubergine and courgettes; stir well, then add tomatoes and season to taste with pepper. Fry gently for 10 minutes, stirring occasionally, then cover and cook gently for 30 minutes, stirring occasionally.

4 Heat the oven to 190C/375F/Gas 5. Cook tagliatelle in boiling, salted water for 8 minutes. Drain well, then rinse in cold water and drain again.

5 Melt 15 g/½ oz butter in pan, add the drained tagliatelle and salt and pepper to taste. Toss well, then turn the noodles into a greased shallow ovenproof dish.

6 Spoon the ratatouille over the tagliatelle. Melt the remaining butter in a pan, then mix in the breadcrumbs and cheese. Sprinkle on top of the dish, then bake for 35-40 minutes until the topping is golden and crisp. Serve hot with garlic bread.

Vegetable brown rice pilaff

Serves 6-8

3 tablespoons corn oil
1 large onion, chopped
1 green pepper, deseeded and diced
1 red pepper, deseeded and diced
100 g/4 oz button mushrooms, quartered
3 celery stalks, trimmed and thinly sliced
1 garlic clove, crushed
225 g/8 oz brown rice
½ teaspoon curry powder
600 ml/1 pint vegetable stock
150 ml/¼ pint tomato juice
salt and freshly ground black pepper
100 g/4 oz frozen sweetcorn kernels
6 spring onions, trimmed and sliced
50 g/2 oz sultanas
50 g/2 oz pine kernels

1 Heat the oil in a large saucepan. Add the chopped onion, green and red peppers, mushrooms, celery and garlic and cook gently for 5 minutes. Stir in the rice and curry powder and fry for 3 minutes, then stir in the stock, tomato juice and salt and pepper to taste.

2 Bring to the boil, then cover and simmer gently for 20 minutes.

3 Add the sweetcorn, spring onions, sultanas and pine kernels. Cover and cook for a further 20 minutes until rice is tender and all liquid is absorbed. Fluff up with a fork and serve hot.

Carrot and watercress mousse

Serves 8-10

225 g/8 oz carrots, chopped
salt and freshly ground black pepper
50 g/2 oz butter
40 g/1½ oz plain flour
600 ml/1 pint vegetable stock
150 ml/¼ pint orange juice
7 teaspoons agar-agar powder
300 ml/½ pint mayonnaise
300 ml/½ pint double cream
1 bunch watercress, stalks trimmed, chopped
4 spring onions, trimmed and chopped
150 ml/¼ pint water
few drops of green food colouring (optional)
vegetable oil, for greasing
TO SERVE (optional)
cherry tomatoes
watercress sprigs

1 Cook the carrots in boiling, salted water for 10-15 minutes until tender. Drain well.
2 Melt 40 g/1½ oz butter in a saucepan, add the flour and cook for 1 minute. Gradually stir in stock and bring to the boil, stirring. Reduce heat and cook for 2 minutes, stirring all the time. Remove from heat and add half the sauce to the carrots.
3 Put the orange juice in a pan, sprinkle over 3 teaspoons agar-agar and bring to the boil, stirring. Cook for 1 minute, stirring all the time. Add to the sauce and carrot mixture and purée in a blender or food processor until smooth. Cool slightly, then whisk in 150 ml/¼ pint mayonnaise and 150 ml/¼ pint double cream. Season to taste.
4 Lightly oil a 1.4-1.7 L/2½-3 pint ring mould. Turn the carrot mixture into the mould and level surface. Leave in refrigerator for 1 hour or until set sufficiently to hold the watercress mixture.
5 At this stage, melt remaining 15 g/½ oz butter in a pan. Add the watercress and spring onions and cook gently for 5 minutes. Add to remaining sauce mixture and blend or process until smooth.
6 Put the water in a pan and sprinkle over the remaining 4 teaspoons agar-agar. Bring to the boil, stirring, then simmer for 1 minute, stirring all the time. Add to the watercress and sauce mixture together with green food colouring, if using. Blend again until smooth. Cool slightly, then whisk in remaining mayonnaise and double cream. Season to taste with salt and pepper.
7 Spoon the mixture over the set carrot layer in the ring mould, level the surface and leave to set in the refrigerator for several hours.
8 To serve: dip the base of the mould into hot water for 1-2 seconds, then invert a serving plate on top. Holding both mould and plate firmly together, invert, giving a sharp shake halfway round. Lift off mould.
9 Fill the centre with cherry tomatoes and watercress sprigs, if wished.

Tomato and cucumber jelly ring

Serves 6-8

1 cucumber, peeled and seeds removed
2 garlic cloves
600 ml/1 pint tomato juice
2 tablespoons lemon juice
2 tablespoons chopped fresh chives
salt and freshly ground black pepper
few drops of Tabasco sauce
1 tablespoon agar-agar powder
TO SERVE
2 ripe avocados
1 tablespoon lemon juice
salt and freshly ground black pepper
cucumber twists

1 Cut up the cucumber and put into a blender or food processor. Add the garlic and tomato juice and process until finely chopped.
2 Turn the mixture into a saucepan, and add the lemon juice, chives, seasoning and Tabasco. Sprinkle over the agar-agar and bring to the boil, stirring. Simmer for 1 minute, stirring all the time.
3 Pour the mixture into a 900 ml/1½ pint fluted ring mould and leave to cool. Chill for at least 2 hours until set.
4 About 30 minutes before serving unmould the jelly: dip the mould into a bowl of hot water for 1-2 seconds, then invert a dampened plate on top. Holding both mould and plate firmly, invert, giving a sharp shake halfway round. Lift off mould.
5 Fill the centre with chopped avocado, sprinkled with the lemon juice and seasoning. Garnish the ring with thin cucumber twists.

Wholewheat spinach and asparagus crêpes

Serves 3-6

100 g/4 oz frozen chopped spinach
100 g/4 oz wholewheat flour
pinch of salt
2 eggs
200 ml/7 fl oz milk
150 ml/¼ pint water
2 tablespoons corn oil
vegetable oil, for greasing
FILLING
65 g/2½ oz butter
1 onion, finely chopped
40 g/1½ oz wholewheat flour
150 ml/¼ pint milk
150 ml/¼ pint water
75 g/3 oz Gruyère cheese, grated
salt and freshly ground black pepper
2 tablespoons single cream
12 cooked asparagus spears
1 teaspoon lemon juice
lime slices, to garnish

1 Cook the spinach following the packet instructions. Drain thoroughly, pressing out any excess moisture; cool.

2 Put the flour and salt into a bowl and make a well in the centre. Add the eggs and gradually stir in half the milk and water. Beat well with a wooden spoon, gradually drawing in the flour to make a smooth batter. Stir in the remaining milk and water and beat well. Stir in the spinach and pour the mixture into a jug.

3 Heat a little oil in a 18-20 cm/7-8 inch frying pan, swirling it over the base and sides of the pan and pour off any excess. Return the pan to the heat and pour in enough spinach batter to coat the base of the pan fairly thickly. Tilt the pan as soon as you pour to help spread the batter, then quickly spread mixture out evenly with the back of a tablespoon to cover the base of the pan.

4 Cook over a high heat for 2-2½ minutes until the underside is golden, then using a fish slice, turn the crêpe over and cook for a further 2-2½ minutes until golden. Remove from pan and place on a flat surface. Fry the remaining batter in the same way to make 6 crêpes in all, adding

more oil to pan between the cooking of each one. (These can be prepared the previous day, stored in the refrigerator in a polythene bag.)

5 Heat the oven to 200C/400F/Gas 6.

6 Make the filling: melt 40 g/1½ oz butter in a saucepan. Add the onion and cook gently for 5 minutes, then stir in the flour and cook for 1 minute, stirring. Gradually stir in the milk and water and bring to the boil, stirring all the time. Reduce the heat and simmer for 2 minutes, stirring. Add the cheese, salt and pepper and cream and remove from heat.

7 Lay crêpes flat on a surface and spread the filling over each one. Fold each crêpe in half, then fold again. Tuck 2 asparagus spears into each folded crêpe. Arrange the crêpes in a greased shallow ovenproof dish.

8 Cover with foil and bake for 20 minutes, then remove the foil and cook for a further 10 minutes until piping hot. Meanwhile melt the remaining butter and add the lemon juice. Drizzle the mixture over the crêpes, garnish with lime slices and serve hot.

Wholewheat spinach and asparagus crêpes

Summer vegetable gougère

Serves 6

CHOUX PASTRY

65 g/2½ oz plain flour

pinch of salt

150 ml/¼ pint water

47 g/1¾ oz butter

2 eggs, beaten

50 g/2 oz Cheddar cheese, diced

FILLING

12 baby carrots

100 g/4 oz French beans, topped, tailed and halved

150 ml/¼ pint boiling water

25 g/1 oz butter

25 g/1 oz plain flour

150 ml/¼ pint milk

100 g/4 oz button mushrooms, sliced

100 g/4 oz fresh or frozen green peas

salt and freshly ground black pepper

50 g/2 oz Cheddar cheese, grated

TO GARNISH

chopped fresh chives

coriander leaves (optional)

1 Heat the oven to 200C/400F/Gas 6. Make the pastry: sift flour and salt on to a piece of greaseproof paper. Put the water and butter in a saucepan and heat gently until the butter has melted. (Do not allow the water to boil before the butter has melted.) Bring to the boil, remove from heat and immediately add the flour, all at once, and stir quickly with a wooden spoon until smooth.

2 Return the pan to a moderate heat for a few moments and beat well until the dough forms a ball and leaves the sides of pan clean. Remove from heat and cool slightly. Gradually add the beaten eggs, beating well after each addition until the mixture forms a shiny dough. Stir in the diced cheese, then spoon mixture around the edge of a greased 23 cm/9 inch ceramic flan dish.

3 Make the filling: cook the carrots and green beans in the boiling water for 7 minutes. Drain well; reserve the liquor and make up to 150 ml/¼ pint with water. Melt the butter in a pan, then stir in the flour and cook for 1 minute. Stir in the reserved cooking liquor and the milk and bring to the boil, stirring. Stir in the mushrooms, carrots, green beans and peas and bring to the boil, stirring. Remove from heat and stir in seasoning

to taste and the grated cheese.

4 Spoon the vegetable mixture into the centre of the dish. Bake for 40-45 minutes until the choux pastry is well risen and golden brown and the vegetables are tender. Sprinkle with chopped chives and garnish with coriander leaves, if using, and serve at once.

Buckwheat courgette and corn crêpes

Serves 8

100 g/4 oz buckwheat flour

pinch of salt

1 egg

150 ml/¼ pint milk

150 ml/¼ pint cold water

1-2 tablespoons corn oil

vegetable oil, for greasing

FILLING

25 g/1 oz butter

100 g/4 oz cooked sweetcorn kernels

2 courgettes, trimmed and grated

4 eggs, separated

75 g/3 oz Cheddar cheese, grated

salt and freshly ground black pepper

½ teaspoon made English mustard

2 teaspoons tomato purée

TO SERVE

1 tablespoon chopped fresh parsley

soured cream

1 Make the pancakes: put the buckwheat flour and salt into a bowl and make a well in the centre. Add the egg and gradually stir in half the milk and water. Beat well with a wooden spoon, gradually drawing in the flour to make a smooth batter. Stir in the remaining milk and water and beat well. Pour into a jug.

2 Heat a little oil in a 15-18 cm/6-7 inch frying pan, swirling it over the base and sides of the pan and pour off any excess. Return the pan to the heat and pour in enough batter to coat the base of the pan thinly, tilting the pan quickly as you pour to help spread the batter evenly.

3 Cook over a high heat for 1½-2 minutes until the underside is golden, then using a palette knife, turn the crêpe over and cook for a further 1½-2 minutes. Remove from the pan and place on a flat surface. Fry the remaining batter in the same way, to make 8 crêpes in all and adding more oil to the pan as necessary. (These can be prepared the previous day and kept stored in refrigerator in a polythene bag.)

4 Heat the oven to 200C/400F/Gas 6.

5 Make the filling: melt 15 g/½ oz of butter in a saucepan. Add the corn and courgettes and cook gently for 3 minutes. Put the egg yolks in a bowl, add the corn and courgette mixture, half the grated cheese, salt and pepper, mustard and tomato purée and mix well. Whisk the egg whites until stiff, then lightly fold into the mixture.

6 Lay the crêpes out flat on a surface and spread the mixture over half of each one, then fold uncovered half over the top. Melt the remaining butter in a pan. Arrange crêpes, slightly overlapping, in a greased shallow ovenproof dish, brushing the surface of each one with melted butter to prevent them sticking together.

7 Cover with foil and bake for 10 minutes; remove foil and cook for a further 10 minutes until the filling has set. Sprinkle with chopped parsley and the remaining grated cheese. Serve hot with soured cream.

Spinach and cheese roulade

Serves 8

500 g/1 lb frozen chopped spinach
3 tablespoons double cream
5 eggs (size 2), separated
salt and freshly ground black pepper
3 tablespoons grated Parmesan cheese
vegetable oil, for greasing
FILLING
225 g/8 oz cottage cheese, sieved
1 tablespoon tomato purée
25 g/1 oz toasted almonds, chopped
4 spring onions, trimmed and sliced thinly
2 tablespoons double cream
salt and freshly ground black pepper

1 Heat the oven to 200C/400F/Gas 6. Grease and line the base and sides of a 33 × 23 cm/13 × 9 inch Swiss roll tin with lightly greased waxed paper.

2 Make the filling: put the cottage cheese into a bowl and add the tomato purée, almonds, spring onions, cream and season to taste with salt and pepper. Mix well together.

3 Cook the frozen spinach following the packet instructions, then drain well, pressing out the excess water. Put spinach into a bowl and add the cream, egg yolks and season to taste with salt and pepper. Mix well together. Whisk the egg whites until stiff, then fold into the spinach mixture.

4 Spread the mixture into the prepared tin and sprinkle with Parmesan cheese. Bake for 10-12 minutes until mixture is cooked through and firm to the touch.

5 Invert the roulade on to a sheet of lightly oiled waxed paper. Remove the tin and carefully peel off the lining paper in strips.

6 Spread the prepared filling over the roll, then carefully roll up, using the paper to help you. Place the roulade on a serving dish and serve hot, cut into chunky slices.

PARTY DESSERTS

As gelatine is an animal product, agar-agar has been used as a setting agent in some of these desserts. Agar-agar comes from seaweed and is available in powder or flake form. You will need a greater quantity if using flakes – 2 tablespoons of flakes will set 500 ml/16 fl oz of liquid compared with just under 2 teaspoons of powder.

Tipsy summer pudding

Serves 8

175 g/6 oz strawberries, hulled

175 g/6 oz raspberries, hulled

175 g/6 oz blackberries, hulled, or use redcurrants or blackcurrants, topped and tailed

3 tablespoons white wine

100 g/4 oz caster sugar

8 trifle sponges

200 ml/7 fl oz double cream

1 teaspoon icing sugar

1 Put the fruits, 2 tablespoons wine and all the caster sugar in a saucepan and bring slowly to the boil. Reduce the heat and cook gently for 5 minutes. Leave to cool.

2 Cut the trifle sponges in half to give 16 thinner pieces. Dip quickly into the juice in the pan and use two-thirds of them to line the base and sides of a 500 g/1 lb, 900 ml/1½ pint capacity, loaf tin. Reserve the remaining one-third.

3 Spoon the fruit mixture into the lined tin, then cover with the reserved dipped sponges. Cover and place a weighted board on top of pudding and chill overnight.

4 Run a knife around the edge of pudding and turn out on to a serving plate. Whip the cream until standing in stiff peaks, then lightly stir in the remaining tablespoon of wine and icing sugar. Serve the pudding sliced, with the cream.

Watermelon sorbet

Serves 8

1 kg/2 lb watermelon flesh

100 g/4 oz granulated sugar

2 teaspoons agar-agar powder

3 tablespoons orange juice

2 egg whites

mint sprigs, to decorate

1 Discard melon seeds, cut up the flesh and purée in a blender or food processor until smooth. Measure the purée - you need 900 ml/1½ pints; make up with water, if necessary.

2 Put 300 ml/½ pint purée in a saucepan with the sugar and bring slowly to the boil. Whisk in the agar-agar and cook for 1 minute, stirring. Add remaining purée and the orange juice and leave to cool, if necessary.

3 Pour the mixture into a metal container and freeze until firm around the edges. Turn mixture into a bowl and break up with a fork. Whisk until smooth. Whisk the egg whites until stiff, then whisk into the mixture.

4 Turn the mixture into a plastic container, cover and freeze until firm.

5 Transfer the sorbet to the refrigerator for 15-30 minutes before serving to allow time for mixture to soften for spooning or scooping.

6 Spoon or scoop the sorbet into serving glass, decorate with mint sprigs and serve with dainty sweet biscuits.

◆ This sorbet is delicious with a little Crème de Cassis poured over just before serving.

Watermelon sorbet

Chocolate kirsch soufflé

Serves 8-10

6 eggs (size 2), separated

175 g/6 oz caster sugar

175 g/6 oz plain chocolate, broken into pieces

6 tablespoons water

4 tablespoons kirsch

3 tablespoons agar-agar powder

300 ml/½ pint double cream

TO DECORATE

chocolate caraque (see below)

icing sugar, for dusting

1 Prepare a 1.1 L/2 pint soufflé dish by wrapping a band of double thickness greaseproof paper around dish, deep enough to stand about 5 cm/2 inches above the rim of dish: tie string firmly under rim of dish.

2 Put the egg yolks and sugar in a heatproof bowl over a saucepan of hot, not boiling, water and whisk until thick and creamy. Remove from heat.

3 Put the chocolate into a heatproof bowl and melt over a saucepan of simmering water. Add to egg and sugar mixture and whisk in well.

4 Heat the water and kirsch until boiling, then whisk in the agar-agar and cook for 1 minute, stirring. Remove from heat and whisk into the still warm chocolate and egg mixture. Whisk well until thoroughly combined. Leave to cool.

5 Whip the cream until softly peaking and whisk the egg whites until stiff. Stir the cold chocolate mixture well, then lightly fold the cream and egg whites into mixture. Pour the mixture into the prepared soufflé dish and level the surface. Set in refrigerator for several hours or overnight.

6 Decorate with chocolate caraque and lightly dust with icing sugar.

◆ To make Chocolate caraque: spread melted, plain chocolate over a baking sheet and leave until set. Hold both ends of a sharp knife almost parallel to the chocolate, slowly push the knife away from you to form thin shavings of chocolate. These will keep in an airtight tin in a cool place.

Variation

◆ Chocolate and orange soufflé: replace the kirsch with the same quantity of unsweetened orange juice and finely grated zest of 1 small orange.

Lime syllabub

Serves 6

300 ml/½ pint double cream

75 g/3 oz caster sugar

3 limes

2 egg whites

18 ratafias

1 Whisk the cream and sugar together until the cream begins to thicken. Finely grate the zest from 2 limes and, using a potato peeler, pare off the zest from the remaining lime and reserve for later. Squeeze out the juice from limes.

2 Add the finely grated zest and lime juice to the cream and whisk until thick and velvety.

3 Whisk the egg whites until stiff and fold into the cream mixture. Put 3 ratafias into each serving glass. Divide the syllabub mixture evenly between glasses. Chill for at least 2 hours.

4 Cut the reserved lime zest into very thin matchstick strips and cook in a little boiling water for 4-5 minutes. Drain and refresh in cold water, then drain well and pat dry on absorbent paper. Sprinkle the lime strips over the syllabubs just before serving.

Passionfruit Pavlova

Serves 8

MERINGUE

3 egg whites (size 2)

200 g/7 oz caster sugar

1 teaspoon cornflour

1 teaspoon vanilla essence

1 teaspoon malt vinegar

FILLING

300 ml/½ pint double cream

2 bananas

2 passionfruit

40 g/1½ oz toasted, flaked almonds

1 Heat the oven to 150C/300F/Gas 2.

2 Whisk the egg whites until stiff. Reserve 1 tablespoon of sugar, then add the remainder to the egg whites, a tablespoon at a time, whisking well after each addition until the mixture is thick and glossy.

3 Mix the cornflour with the reserved sugar and gradually whisk into the meringue. Add the vanilla essence and vinegar and whisk well until the meringue is very stiff, smooth and glossy.

4 Spoon the meringue mixture on to a 23 cm/9 inch ovenproof serving plate and spread out with a palette knife to an 18 cm/7 inch even round shape.

5 Reduce oven temperature to 140C/275F/Gas 1 and cook for 1 hour until lightly coloured and crisp on the outside. Switch off oven, open oven door and leave meringue inside until cool.

6 About 1½ hours before serving, prepare the filling: whip the cream until thick and spoon into the centre of Pavlova. Slice the bananas and arrange over the cream. Scoop out the pulp and black seeds from the passionfruit and spoon over the banana. Scatter the surface with toasted, flaked almonds. Serve within 1½ hours of assembling.

◆ Pavlova will tend to crack and sink slightly on cooling, however this is quite usual and won't show once filled with cream and fruit topping.

Variation

◆ Use any fresh fruit of your choice for topping the Pavlova, such as raspberries, strawberries, redcurrants or pineapple.

Raspberry party meringues

Serves 6

2 egg whites

100 g/4 oz caster sugar

vegetable oil for, greasing

FILLING

300 ml/½ pint double cream

few drops of vanilla essence

1-2 teaspoons icing sugar

225 g/8 oz raspberries, hulled

1 Mark six 6.5 cm/2½ inch circles on the underside of a sheet of waxed paper and place on a lightly greased baking sheet. Heat the oven to 110C/225F/Gas ¼.

2 Whisk the egg whites until stiff. Add half the sugar and whisk again until stiff and glossy. Lightly fold the remaining sugar into the meringue.

3 Spoon the mixture into a piping bag fitted with a large star nozzle. Pipe the mixture on to the marked circles, starting from the centre and working out to edges, in a swirl to fill the circle. Pipe remaining meringue into six rosettes (to form 'hats' for meringue circles later on).

4 Bake for 6 hours or overnight.

5 Remove dry, crisp meringues carefully from the paper and leave to cool on a wire rack for 10 minutes. (These can now be stored in an airtight tin for several weeks.)

6 Just before serving, whip the cream with the vanilla essence and icing sugar to taste until stiff. Put the mixture into a piping bag fitted with a large star nozzle and pipe two-thirds of the cream on to the meringue circles. Top each one with raspberries. Pipe the remaining cream on to the bases of meringue rosettes, then place a rosette in the centre of each raspberry-topped meringue. Press down lightly. Serve within 30 minutes of assembling.

Variations

◆ Tint the meringue mixture pale pink if wished, using 1-2 drops red food colouring.

◆ Sprinkle piped, uncooked meringues with chopped nuts before cooking.

◆ Replace raspberries with strawberries or peeled, sliced fresh peaches.

Chocolate rum gateau

Serves 8-10

150 g/5 oz plain flour
25 g/1 oz cocoa
pinch of salt
2 teaspoons baking powder
150 g/5 oz dark soft brown sugar
40 g/1½ oz ground almonds
2 eggs, separated
6 tablespoons corn oil
150 ml/¼ pint soured cream
½ teaspoon vanilla essence
vegetable oil, for greasing
RUM SYRUP
150 g/5 oz granulated sugar
250 ml/8 fl oz water
4 tablespoons dark rum
2 tablespoons orange juice
DECORATION
whipped cream
chocolate thins, buttons or dragees

1 Well grease a 1.7 L/3 pint fluted ring tin or gugelhopf mould. Heat oven to 180C/350F/Gas 4.
2 Sift the flour, cocoa, salt and baking powder in to a bowl and add the sugar and ground almonds. Mix the egg yolks with the oil, soured cream and vanilla essence. Add to flour mixture and beat well to form a smooth batter.
3 Whisk the egg whites until stiff, then fold into the cake mixture. Pour the mixture into the prepared tin and level the surface.
4 Bake for 1 hour or until cooked, covering surface with foil, if necessary, to prevent over-browning. Turn out on to a wire rack and cool.
5 Make the syrup: put the sugar and water in a saucepan and heat gently until the sugar dissolves. Bring to the boil and boil for 5 minutes. Remove from heat. Add rum and orange juice.
6 Put the cold cake on a plate and slowly pour the hot syrup over the top. Leave to soak for 1 hour, spooning up syrup from plate and pouring over cake occasionally until syrup is absorbed.
7 Transfer the cake to a serving plate and decorate with whipped cream and chocolate thins, buttons or dragees.

Brandy snaps with coffee cream

Makes 12

50 g/2 oz butter
50 g/2 oz demerara sugar
50 g/2 oz golden syrup
50 g/2 oz plain flour
pinch of salt
½ teaspoon ground ginger
½ teaspoon lemon juice
vegetable oil, for greasing
COFFEE CREAM
2 teaspoons instant coffee granules
1 teaspoon boiling water
300 ml/½ pint double cream
1 teaspoon icing sugar

1 Heat the oven to 160C/325F/Gas 3.
2 Put the butter, sugar and syrup in a saucepan and heat gently until the butter has melted and the sugar dissolved. Leave to cool slightly.
3 Sift the flour, salt and ginger into the mixture, add the lemon juice and mix well.
4 Put teaspoonfuls of mixture on well greased baking sheets, spacing them well apart to allow for spreading. Bake (one sheet at a time) for 10 minutes until golden. Leave to cool on the baking sheet for 2 minutes, then remove from the sheet with a palette knife, turn over and roll around the handle of a wooden spoon. Leave until set in shape. (These can be stored in an airtight tin for up to 2 weeks.)
5 Just before serving, dissolve the coffee in the boiling water; leave to cool. Whip the cream until stiff, then stir in the icing sugar and coffee mixture. Put coffee cream into a piping bag, fitted with a small star tube and pipe mixture into both ends of the brandy snaps. Serve at once.

Variation

◆ Crush 75 g/3 oz fresh strawberries or raspberries and fold into sweetened whipped cream. Transfer the mixture to a piping bag, fitted with a 1 cm/½ inch plain tube and pipe the mixture into the brandy snaps.

Brandy snaps with coffee cream

Apricot hazelnut vacherin

Serves 8-10

4 egg whites

100 g/4 oz light soft brown sugar

100 g/4 oz caster sugar

100 g/4 oz ground hazelnuts

FILLING

100 g/ 4 oz dried apricots

150 ml/¼ pint orange juice

25 g/1 oz soft brown sugar

2 tablespoons cold water

300 ml/½ pint double cream

DECORATION

50 g/2 oz plain chocolate

150 ml/¼ pint double cream

toasted hazelnuts

1 Mark the underside of 3 sheets of waxed paper with an 18 cm/7 inch circle and place each sheet on a lightly greased baking sheet. Heat the oven to 160C/325F/Gas 3.

2 Whisk the egg whites until stiff, then gradually whisk in the sugars, a little at a time, until the mixture is thick and glossy. Fold the hazelnuts into the meringue.

3 Divide the mixture evenly between the 3 circles and spread out with a palette knife. Bake for 35-40 minutes until lightly golden and crisp on the outside. Remove from the oven, leave to cool, then remove lining papers.

4 Meanwhile, put the apricots in a saucepan with the orange juice and sugar. Cover and cook gently for 20 minutes until tender and almost all the liquid is absorbed (it will be very thick and syrupy).

5 Put mixture into a blender or food processor with the water and blend to form a very thick, smooth purée, adding a little extra water, if necessary to blend successfully. Leave to cool.

6 About 1 hour before serving, whip the cream until softly peaking and fold in the thick apricot purée. Put one meringue round on a serving plate and spread with half the apricot cream. Place second meringue round on top and spread with the remaining apricot cream. Top with the third meringue round. Press down lightly.

7 Break the chocolate into pieces and put into a polythene bag and melt it in a bowl over hot water. Snip off a tiny piece of the bag at one corner and, using a slow back and forth movement, drizzle the melted chocolate over the surface of the vacherin.

8 Whip the cream until softly peaking. Put into a piping bag fitted with a plain nozzle and pipe swirls of whipped cream around top edge of vacherin, then decorate each one with a toasted hazelnut.

Exotic melon basket

Serves 8

1 large ripe honeydew melon

100 g/4 oz strawberries, hulled and sliced

2 kiwi fruits, peeled, quartered and sliced

8 black or green grapes, halved and pips removed

½ × 310 g/11 oz can lychees, halved

2 nectarines, stoned and sliced

SYRUP

juice of 1 small orange

2 tablespoons lychee syrup

1 passionfruit

I Cut a thin lengthways sliver from one side of melon to give a flat base so it sits firmly. Make handle: from the top, make one vertical cut 1 cm/½ inch from the centre to halfway down the melon; make a similar cut 1 cm/½ inch to other side. Using a sharp, pointed knife, cut the melon horizontally from the downward cuts, and in a zig-zag motion, around melon on each side. Lift the two sections away from basket, leaving a 2.5 cm/1 inch wide handle in the centre of melon.

2 Discard melon seeds from the two sections and from the basket. Carefully scoop out the melon flesh, using a melon baller, taking care not to damage the basket. Put the melon balls into a bowl and add the remaining fruits.

3 Make the syrup: mix the orange juice and lychee syrup. Scoop out the passionfruit pulp and seeds and add to the syrup. Pour over fruits and stir gently.

4 Spoon the mixture back into the basket. Cover and serve chilled with pouring cream, or yoghurt, if preferred.

Redcurrant cheesecake

Serves 8-10

BASE

50 g/2 oz soft margarine

50 g/2 oz caster sugar

1 egg, beaten

65 g/2 ½ oz self-raising flour

½ teaspoon baking powder

FILLING

175 g/6 oz cream cheese

50 g/2 oz caster sugar

2 eggs, separated

finely grated zest of 1 lemon

3 tablespoons lemon juice

3 tablespoons water

5 teaspoons agar-agar powder

150 ml/¼ pint natural yoghurt

150 ml/¼ pint double cream

TOPPING

175-225 g/6-8 oz redcurrants, topped and tailed

75 g/3 oz caster sugar

4 tablespoons water

4 teaspoons arrowroot

1 tablespoon lemon juice

1 Grease and line the base and sides of a 20 cm/8 inch loose-bottomed deep cake tin with grease-proof paper, allowing the paper to come 2.5 cm/1 inch above the rim of tin. Heat the oven to 180C/350F/Gas 4.

2 Make the base: put margarine, sugar, egg, flour and baking powder in a bowl and beat well for 2 minutes using a wooden spoon (or for only 1 minute if using an electric mixer). Spoon into the prepared tin and level the surface.

3 Bake for 20 minutes until risen and lightly golden. Leave to cool in the tin.

4 Make the filling: beat the cream cheese with sugar until soft and creamy, then add the egg yolks and lemon zest and beat until smooth.

5 Heat the lemon juice and water until boiling, then whisk in the agar-agar and cook for 1 minute, stirring. (The mixture will be very thick.) Remove from the heat and leave to cool slightly.

6 Whisk the agar-agar mixture into the cream cheese mixture and then whisk in the yoghurt, whisking until mixture is smooth and thoroughly combined. Whip cream until softly peaking and fold into the mixture. Whisk the egg whites until stiff, then fold into the mixture. Whisk very lightly to combine all the ingredients, if necessary.

7 Pour the mixture over the cold cake in the tin and level the surface. Leave to set in the refrigerator for 3-4 hours.

8 Make the topping: put the redcurrants, sugar and water in a saucepan and cook gently for 5 minutes. Blend the arrowroot with the lemon juice, add to the pan and boil for 2 minutes, stirring all the time. Cool until lukewarm, then spoon over the top of the cheesecake. Leave to set for 1-2 hours.

9 Remove the cheescake from the tin, using the paper to help you lift the cake. Remove the greaseproof paper and place the cheesecake on a serving dish.

Variations

◆ Use blackcurrants instead of redcurrants, if preferred.

◆ Replace the yoghurt in the filling with the same quantity of soured cream.

Strawberry custard flan

Serves 8

FRENCH FLAN PASTRY

175 g/6 oz plain flour

pinch of salt

75 g/3 oz butter, softened

75 g/3 oz caster sugar

1 egg yolk

1 tablespoon cold water

few drops of vanilla essence

FILLING

3 egg yolks

50 g/2 oz caster sugar

25 g/1 oz plain flour

300 ml/½ pint milk

1 tablespoon cornflour

1 tablespoon water

25 g/1 oz butter

few drops of vanilla essence

TOPPING

500 g/1 lb strawberries, hulled and sliced

2 tablespoons redcurrant jelly

2 teaspoons lemon juice

1 Make the pastry: sift the flour and salt into a bowl and make a well in the centre. Add the butter, sugar, egg yolk, water and vanilla essence and rub in until mixture forms a fairly soft dough. Knead gently, then cover and chill for 1 hour.

2 Make the filling: put the egg yolks and sugar in a bowl and beat until smooth and creamy. Stir in the flour and mix well. Heat the milk until hot, but not boiling, and gradually stir into the egg mixture. Return the mixture to the pan and bring to the boil slowly over a low heat, stirring all the time. Blend the cornflour with the water, add to pan and cook for 2 minutes, stirring all the time until custard is slightly thickened and smooth. Remove from the heat and beat in the butter and vanilla essence. Cover with damp greaseproof paper and leave to cool.

3 Heat the oven to 190C/375F/Gas 5.

4 Roll out the pastry on a lightly floured surface large enough to line the base and sides of a 23 cm/9 inch fluted flan tin, set on a baking sheet. Trim edges and prick base all over with a fork. Line with greaseproof paper and fill with baking beans. Bake in the oven for 10 minutes. Remove the paper and beans and cook for a further 7-8 minutes until cooked through and golden. Remove from the oven and leave to cool.

5 Fill the cold flan case with the custard mixture and level the surface. Arrange the strawberries on top of the custard. Heat the redcurrant jelly and lemon juice together until smooth and melted. Boil for 3 minutes, cool slightly, then spoon over the strawberries to form a glaze. Leave to set before serving.

Variation

◆ Use stoned, fresh cherries instead of strawberries for the topping and add a few drops of kirsch to the custard instead of vanilla essence.

Strawberry custard flan

Tropical fruit mille feuille

Serves 8

ROUGH PUFF PASTRY

225 g/8 oz plain flour

pinch of salt

150 g/5 oz butter, cut into walnut-sized pieces

150 ml/¼ pint cold water

1 teaspoon lemon juice

FILLING

5-6 tablespoons apricot jam

200 ml/7 fl oz double cream, whipped

3 kiwi fruit, peeled and sliced

3 slices fresh pineapple, skin and centre core removed and flesh cut into pieces

1 mango, peeled and stone removed and flesh cut into pieces

12 strawberries, hulled and sliced

1 Make the pastry: sift the flour and salt into a bowl and add the pieces of butter. Stir in the water and lemon juice and mix gently to form a dough (take care not to break up the butter).

2 Knead very lightly and shape into a rectangular block. Roll out on a lightly floured surface to a strip about 1 cm/½ inch thick, 10 cm/4 inches wide and 30 cm/12 inches long, keeping edges straight as you roll by patting to keep the shape.

3 Mark the pastry into 3 equal portions and fold the bottom one-third up and over centre one-third, then fold top one-third down to cover both these layers. Seal the edges together using a rolling pin, then give the pastry a quarter turn clockwise. Repeat the process 4 more times. Wrap in cling film and refrigerate for 15 minutes.

4 Heat the oven to 220C/425F/Gas 7. Roll out the pastry thinly on a lightly floured surface to a 38 × 25 cm/15 × 10 inch rectangle. Trim the edges to neaten, then cut into three, 12.5 × 25 cm/5 × 10 inch strips. Place on dampened baking sheets and bake in the oven for 15 minutes until well risen and golden. Cool on a wire rack.

5 About 1 hour before serving, spread each pastry strip with jam and top with whipped cream. Cover each layer with an assortment of fruits. Place one layer on a serving plate, then top with the remaining 2 layers. Served chilled.

Variation

◆ Substitute any soft summer fruits for the ones used here.

Mint and chocolate chip ice cream

Serves 6-8

300 ml/½ pint single cream

6 egg yolks

100 g/4 oz caster sugar

few drops of oil of peppermint or peppermint essence

2-3 drops of green food colouring (optional)

300 ml/½ pint double cream

75 g/3 oz plain chocolate chips

crisp fan wafers, to serve

1 Heat the single cream until hot, but not boiling. Put the egg yolks in a heatproof bowl and pour the cream on to the egg yolks, stirring. Add the sugar and place the bowl over a saucepan of simmering water. Whisk or stir until mixture coats the back of a wooden spoon.

2 Strain the mixture into a bowl, then leave to cool. Add the peppermint oil or essence and green food colouring, if using.

3 Whip the double cream until softly peaking and fold into the cold custard. Turn the mixture into a 1 kg/2 lb, 1.7L/3 pint capacity, loaf tin. Cover and freeze until the sides of ice cream begin to set.

4 Turn sides of mixture to the middle and mix well with a fork, then stir in the chocolate chips. Re-cover and freeze again until firm.

5 Transfer the ice cream to the main compartment of the refrigerator about 30 minutes before serving to allow time for the mixture to soften for scooping. Serve with crisp fan wafers.

Strawberry Charlotte

Serves 12

175 g/6 oz unsalted butter, softened

100 g/4 oz caster sugar

grated zest and juice of 1 orange

few drops of almond essence

100 g/4 oz ground almonds

300 ml/½ pint dry white wine

450 ml/¾ pint double cream

2 packets sponge fingers

350 g/12 oz strawberries, hulled

butter, for greasing

1 Grease the base of an 18 cm/7 inch deep loose-bottomed cake tin and line with grease-proof paper; grease the lining paper.
2 In a large mixing bowl, beat the butter, sugar, orange zest and almond essence together until light and fluffy. Gradually beat in the ground almonds alternately with 100 ml/3½ fl oz of the wine. Do not add the wine too quickly or the mixture may curdle.
3 Whip 300 ml/½ pint of the cream until it forms soft peaks, then fold into the almond mixture.
4 Mix the remaining wine with the orange juice in a large bowl. Trim the sponge fingers so that they are the same height as the tin. Reserve the trimmings. Dip each sponge finger very quickly into the wine and orange mixture and use to line the sides of the cake tin in a single layer, placing the rounded untrimmed end upwards and the sugar-coated side outwards.
5 Quickly soak any remaining sponge fingers, together with the reserved trimmed ends, in the wine and orange mixture. Reserve 100 g/4 oz of the strawberries, slice the rest.
6 Spread one-third of the almond mixture over the base of the prepared tin. Cover with half the sliced strawberries and half the remaining sponge fingers and trimmed ends. Repeat these layers once more, finishing with the remaining third of almond mixture.
7 Place a piece of greased grease proof paper over the top. Cover with a small plate and place a weight on top.
8 Refrigerate for at least 4 hours, or preferably overnight until the mixture is quite firm.
9 Remove the weight and paper. Place an in-verted plate on top of the tin. Holding the plate and tin firmly, invert giving a sharp shake halfway round. Lift off the tin.
10 Slice all but one of the reserved strawberries. Arrange the slices over the top and around the bottom edge of the Charlotte; place the whole one in the centre. Whip the remaining cream until it forms soft peaks and pipe decoratively around the top and bottom edges. Chill until ready to serve.

Three-berry mousse

Serves 8

500 g/1 lb mixed berry fruits (strawberries, raspberries, blackberries), hulled

100 g/4 oz caster sugar

1 tablespoon lemon juice

3 tablespoons cold water

1 tablespoon agar-agar powder

150 ml/¼ pint double cream

2 egg whites

SAUCE

350 g/12 oz raspberries, hulled

6 tablespoons icing sugar

1 Place the fruits in a saucepan with the sugar and lemon juice. Cook over a gentle heat for 10 minutes. Press through a sieve and return the purée to the pan. Add the water and bring to the boil. Whisk in the agar-agar and boil for 1 minute, whisking all the time. Remove from heat and leave to cool.
2 Whip the cream until softly peaking and whisk the egg whites until stiff. Fold both into the cold fruit purée. Pour the mixture into a serving bowl and chill until set.
3 Make the sauce: either press the raspberries through a sieve or purée them in a blender or food processor. Stir in the icing sugar. Pour into a serving jug and chill until required. Serve the mousse with the sauce handed separately.

Variation

◆ Use only one fruit, if preferred, to make a strawberry or raspberry mousse.

DRINKS

Hot days call for cool drinks and this chapter includes both alcoholic and non-alcoholic drinks to suit all occasions, from sophisticated summer cocktails to a healthy chilled vegetable cup.

The Iced vegetable cup (see page 118) can be served for summer lunches or for a non-alcoholic party drink, or for a more sophisticated non-alcoholic punch try China tea punch (see page 119) a beautifully refreshing, delicately-flavoured punch. Children will love the flavour of homemade Orange barley (see page 118) and it is just the thing to take on a picnic.

Mid-summer spritzer (see page 122) is a pretty, pale pink wine drink that's suitable for lunchtime or evening parties, while the Summer champagne cocktail (see page 120) is an elegant drink for more formal occasions.

Brunches and barbecues are both popular in the summer and there are drinks to suit both events. Brunch cup royale is a delicious drink made with freshly squeezed orange juice, brandy and rosé wine. Spiced claret cup is a full-flavoured, yet light, drink which is perfect for serving with barbecued food.

Float slices of fruit such as strawberries, mango or kiwi fruit or whole raspberries in the punch bowl or serving jug. Or add sprigs of herbs or flowers such as nasturtium or borage.

Ice cubes

Make sure you have plenty of ice cubes – it's surprising how quickly they melt in hot weather. Freeze several trays of cubes, then pack them into freezer bags, spraying with soda water to prevent them sticking together. If you want crushed ice, wrap the ice in a clean tea towel and smash it with a hammer.

Decorative ice cubes turn any drink into a party special. Put twists of orange or lemon zest, cherries, strawberries, small cubes of pineapple, mint leaves or borage flowers into ice cube trays, fill with water – or fruit juice, if preferred – and then freeze them.

Mango lassi

Serves 4

1 mango, about 250 g/9 oz

275 ml/9 fl oz natural yoghurt

2-4 tablespoons caster sugar

4 ice cubes

1 teaspoon very finely chopped pistachio nuts, to decorate (optional)

1 Skin, halve and stone the mango and purée in a blender or food processor with the yoghurt and sugar to taste. (You may need to purée it in 2 batches if using a blender.)
2 Put an ice cube into each of 4 tall glass tumblers and pour the mixture on top.
3 Sprinkle chopped pistachio nuts over the top and serve at once while the drinks are cold and very frothy.

Variation

◆ Omit the mango, increase the amount of yoghurt to 350 ml/12 fl oz and add 300 ml/½ pint ice cold water. Blend the mixture half at a time and decorate with crushed cumin seeds instead of pistachio nuts.

China tea punch